James Aspinall

Liverpool a few Years since

Third Edition

James Aspinall

Liverpool a few Years since
Third Edition

ISBN/EAN: 9783744728645

Printed in Europe, USA, Canada, Australia, Japan

Cover: Foto ©ninafisch / pixelio.de

More available books at **www.hansebooks.com**

LIVERPOOL

A FEW YEARS SINCE:

BY

AN OLD STAGER.

THIRD EDITION.

LIVERPOOL:
ADAM HOLDEN, 48, CHURCH STREET.

1885.

CONTENTS.

CHAPTER I.

Liverpool fifty years since. Goree warehouses. The docks. Extent of the town. Ships in dock. Ships for sea. Outward bound 1

CHAPTER II.

War. The old "Princess." The Press-gangs—their unpopularity—Jack's race for life 6

CHAPTER III.

Captain Colquitt. Convoys. Privateers. Dublin packets. The deserts of Cheshire 12

CHAPTER IV.

Volunteers. Captain Bolton. The Marquis of Londonderry. General Benson. General Fisher 18

CHAPTER V.

Prince William of Gloucester. The Prince of Wales. The Duke of Clarence. Scene at the Mayor's dinner 23

CHAPTER VI.

Old stagers—Dr. Currie, John Foster, Dr. Brandreth, Sir William Barton, John Bridge Aspinall, John Bolton 29

CHAPTER VII.

Moses Benson. Fashionables. Military beaux. Major Brackenbury. Thomas Leyland. Pudsey Dawson 35

CHAPTER VIII.

Fletcher Raincock. James Clark. The Recorder non-suited. George Rowe. Jack Shaw. The old Corporation .. 41

CHAPTER IX.

Sir George Dunbar. Tom Dunbar. Thomas Wilson. Edward Houghton. Mr. Black's white wig. Roger Leigh .. 47

CHAPTER X.

Joseph Leigh. Shakespeare Tom. William Harper. Bamber Gascoigne 54

CHAPTER XI.

Society. Sets. Roscoe—how appreciated. Anecdote. Dr. Shepherd 61

CHAPTER XII.

Sir Joseph Birch. Arthur Heywood. Tom Lowndes. Colonel Nicholson. Rushton. Captain Crowe. Night Action. Peter Tyrer 68

CHAPTER XIII.

William James. Silvester Richmond. Anecdotes. Joseph Daltera. Puns. Jokes. Sermon 76

CHAPTER XIV.

Practical Jokes and Jokers. Committee of Taste—their doings and misdoings. Quarrel with Mr. Staniforth—how settled. Their Chairman. Improvement of the present age .. 83

Contents.

CHAPTER XV.

The old tower in Water-street. Committee of Taste again—more of their pranks. William Wallace Currie—his character and writings 90

CHAPTER XVI.

Sir John Gladstone—his character. Ottiwell Wood. Judge Littledale. General D'Aguilar. Devaynes, the conjurer .. 97

CHAPTER XVII.

Old watchmen—tricks played upon them. Pigtails. The last and very last of the pigtails. Hair powder. Barbers ruined. Marshall Blucher—preparing for the Battle of Leipsic 104

CHAPTER XVIII.

The old Corporation—their exclusive spirit—their doings. Management of public affairs. Anecdotes. Corporation dinners—county guests. Honest John Watkins, and his defeat at Waterloo 113

CHAPTER XIX.

The Clergy. Blair's sermons. The Rev. Thomas Kidd. The Rev. Thomas Moss. Anecdotes. The Bottle and the Wood. Chat Moss 122

CHAPTER XX.

Rector Roughsedge. Anecdotes. The Bishop astonishing the Clergy. The Rector's one joke. St. George's Church. The Mayor's Procession. Maternal discipline. After Church. Lord Street. The Athenæum steps 130

CHAPTER XXI.

Jonas. Mr. Pitt. The Duke. Archdeacon Brooks. The Rev. James Hamer. Dr. Hodgson—in Liverpool—in Oxford—his character, career, and brilliant talents 138

Contents.

CHAPTER XXII.

An Election. Parties in the Town and Council. General Tarleton. Old Freemen. General Gascoigne. Bamber Gascoigne. Conscience ... : 145

CHAPTER XXIII.

Shops. Danson. Shower bath. The Liverpool Hunt. Peter Carter and his gray horse. Abraham Lowe, the huntsman. Cheshire Squires. Sir Peter Warburton. Sir Harry Mainwaring 154

CHAPTER XXIV.

Old Coaches. Macadam. Coachmen. The Umpire. The Bang-up. Pleasures of travelling on the old roads. Hours kept by our grandfathers and grandmothers. Visiting. Sedan Cahirs. Routs. Going out and going home 164

CHAPTER XXV.

Theatres—the managers—actors—singers. Elliston. Lord Nelson. George Bailey. Abolition of the Slave Trade. Liverpool ruined. Liverpool revived. Conclusion 172

PREFACE TO THE THIRD EDITION.

THIS little volume has been twice published, and this issue of it is in ready response to the "third time of asking" by an appreciating public, largely, as we imagine, made up of families associated in some way or other with "Old Liverpool" as it appeared in the earlier part of the present century.

The traditions of the "Good Old Town" naturally have an interest to many of us who are also quite able and equally willing to estimate at their full value the modern development and rapid progress of the "New City."

"The inaudible and noiseless foot of time"

passes rapidly on, but even the days that are spent may

"As withered roses yield a late perfume,"

and so give us often very bright and happy retrospects.

Perhaps it may soon be a self-inspired and pleasurable task for someone to take up the thread of the "Old Stager's" story, and bring it down to the present time. Meanwhile, let us hope that the kindly enterprise of the publisher may be rewarded by a rapid demand for this little book, at once of real interest to old Liverpool families and at the same time so simple and sketchy in its style as to give it no place whatever in the "records" of the community.

CLARKE ASPINALL.

LIVERPOOL, 1885.

PREFACE TO THE SECOND EDITION.

IN the year 1852, *Liverpool a Few Years Since*, by "An Old Stager," was republished in "a more abiding form" than it had previously assumed in the columns of the *Liverpool Albion*. The little book sold off rapidly, notwithstanding its being somewhat expensive, as compared with the wonderfully cheap publications of the day, and it is now out of print. It has many a time and oft been suggested that a further and cheaper issue would be acceptable to the Liverpool public, The publisher has, therefore, assumed the responsibility of the present issue; and, learning that such was his intention, I have ventured to "preface" the original preface by a word or two in explanation of the circumstances and surroundings under which the Author penned these sketches.

It is scarcely imparting information, to make known the simple truth that the "Old Stager" in question was none other than the late Rev. James Aspinall, M.A. Oxon, at one time Incumbent of St. Michael's Church, and more recently officiating at St. Luke's, and afterwards transferred to the Crown Rectory of Althorpe in Lincolnshire, where he continued to reside until his death in 1861. The "Old Stager" was always a man of great activity of mind and body, and could never be idle. Every moment of his time was turned to some account; and thus the very remote sphere of his parochial and magisterial duties in Lincolnshire never induced the slightest dulness or discontent. With a Church, and a Chapel of Ease three or four miles off, to serve, and with a tolerably large parish to care for, the "Old Stager" was not without considerable clerical duty; and, added to this, he most unwillingly undertook the responsibilities of the magisterial office. Notwithstanding the avocations thus indicated, time was always found for literary pursuits, for receiving and imparting knowledge, for refreshing and renewing his powers of mind, in order to the successful communication, either by voice or pen, of his thoughts and ideas to his neighbours and to the general public. Amid the many written utterances of the "Old Stager's" ready and comprehensive mind, we must enumerate these notes upon men and things in our good old town, penned with very considerable pleasure to their writer, as being the jottings down of his own personal experiences and recollections of a place and of a people very deeply rooted in the affections of this true son of Liverpool.

We well remember the bright and genial countenance of the "Old Stager," as he thought aloud upon his old and early associations. Liverpool was his home, as against all other homes. His father had been its chief magistrate so long ago as 1803. His sons, or some of them, had adopted it as their abiding place; and thus, for several generations, this thriving community seemed to the " Old Stager " to smile upon him and upon his belongings, and as a consequence, not at all unnatural, the " Old Stager " felt a devotion to the town, and towards its inhabitants, which kept it and them ever in his grateful remembrance.

C. A.

LIVERPOOL, *January*, 1869.

PREFACE.

THE original intention of the Author was to amuse the younger readers of the *Albion*, by dashing off a few sketches of "men and things," as he recollects them in Liverpool a few years since. For this purpose all that was worth telling, he thought, might be comprised in about two papers, or chapters. The public, however, like hungry Oliver Twist, revelling on the thin workhouse gruel, flatteringly asked for "more"; and with this request he, not being of a nature akin to that of Mr. Bumble, has willingly complied to the extent of his ability. Nor is this all for which the naughty public is to be held responsible. The chapters having been spun out to the length which they now occupy, greedy Oliver again cries out for "more," and demands that, instead of being left to die out, and be forgotten, as the ephemeral occupants of the columns of a newspaper, they shall be collected, and re-published in a more abiding form; and once more our good nature triumphs over our prudence, and we comply. Under such circumstances, the writer of these sketches and reminiscences neither courts nor deprecates criticism; his only object in perpetrating these "trifles light as air" was, he repeats, to set before the rising generation a picture of the "good" old town, at the commencement of the present century, and to show them how "men and manners," and customs and fashions, have changed since the times in which their grandfathers "ruled the roast," and were the heroes of the day. In working out this design, the Author has had neither dates nor memoranda to refer to, but has trusted entirely to his own powers of recollection, even as far back as the period when he reached the mature age of six years! It is satisfactory, however, to add that, although he has painted wholly from memory, no one has yet disputed the accuracy of any of the characters which he has drawn, the events which he has related, or the anecdotes which he has revived. This may be fairly assumed as a testimony in favour of their correctness. For the rest, he has only once more to say, with Horace, "*Non meus hic sermo,*" &c.; that is, our reappearance is no fault of our own. Oliver Twist "has done it all," and must bear the blame.

LIVERPOOL, *October*, 1852.

Liverpool a Few Years Since.

CHAPTER I.

E are not great at statistics. We do not pretend to be accurate to an hour in dates, chronology, and so forth. We write, indeed, entirely from memory, and therefore may perhaps occasionally go wrong in fixing "the hour for the man, and the man for the hour," as we dot down a few of our recollections of the "good old town of Liverpool," from the time when we cast off our swaddling clothes, crept out of our cradle, opened our eyes, and began to exercise our reasoning powers on men and things as in those days they presented themselves to our view. We think that our memory has a faint glimmering of the illuminations which took place when peace was made with Napoleon, in 1801. We also remember being called out of our bed to gaze at the terrible flames when the Goree warehouses were burnt down, and how we crept out of the house at day dawn, and rushed to see the blazing mass and all its tottering ruins in dangerous proximity.

It might only have happened yesterday, so vividly is the scene impressed upon our mind. But what was Liverpool in those days of early hours, pigtails, routs and hair-powder?

The docks ended with George's at one extremity and the Queen's at the other. There was a battery near the latter and another near the former. Farther north was a large fort of some thirty guns, and half-way towards Bootle, a smaller one with nine. The town hardly on one side extended beyond Colquitt-street. The greater part of Upper Duke-street was unbuilt. Cornwallis-street, the large house which Mr. Morrall erected, the ground on which St. Michael's Church stands, all were fields at the time of which we speak. There was a picturesque-looking mill at the top of Duke-street, and behind Rodney-street we had a narrow lane, with a high bank overgrown with roses. Russell-street, Seymour-street, and all beyond were still free from bricks. Lime-street was bounded by a field, in which many a time we watched rough lads chasing cocks on Shrove Tuesday for a prize, the competitors having their hands tied behind them, and catching at the victims with their mouths. Edge-hill, Everton, and Kirkdale were villages, as yet untouched by the huge Colossus which has since absorbed them and transmuted them into suburbs. What pilgrimages we children used to achieve to the second of these places, the very Mecca of our affections, that we might expend our small cash upon genuine Molly Bushell's toffee. And what wonderful tales we heard from our nurses and companions about Prince Rupert's

Cottage,—only lately demolished by some modern Goth, under the plea of improvement! And then we crept on to peep at the old beacon at San Domingo, thinking what a clever device it was to rouse and alarm the country, never dreaming in our young heads of telegraphs, and electric telegraphs, and other inventions, which have now superseded the rude makeshifts of our forefathers. And what a grand house we thought Mr. Harper's, at Everton, now turned into barracks. And Hope-street, now so central, then gave no hopes of existence. It was country altogether. At one end of it were two gentlemen's seats, inhabited by the families of Corrie and Thomas, and far removed from the smoke and bustle of the town.

But go we back to the docks. There were no steamers in those days to tow out our vessels. The wind ruled supreme, without a rival. The consequence was, that when, after a long stretch of contrary winds, a change took place, and a favourable breeze set in, a whole fleet of ships would at once be hauled out of dock, and start upon their several voyages. It was a glorious spectacle. It was the delight of our younger days to be present on all such occasions. How we used to fly about, sometimes watching the dashing American ships as they left the King's and Queen's Docks, and sometimes taking a peep at the coasters in the Salthouse Dock, or at the African traders in the Old Dock, since filled up, at the instigation of some goose anxious to emulate the fame of the man who set fire to the Temple at Ephesus. This fatal blunder it was which first gave a wrong direction to our docks, stretching them out northwards and southwards *in extenso*, instead of centralising and keeping them together. But we must not moralise. We are at the dock side, or on the pierhead. The tide is rising, the wind is favourable, " The sea, the sea, the open sea," is the word with all. What bustle and confusion! What making fast and casting off of ropes! How the captains shout! How the men swear! How the dock-masters rush about! What horrible " confusion worse confounded" seems to prevail! And yet there is method in all this seeming madness. Order will presently come out of all this apparent chaos. The vessels pass through the dockgates. Meat and bread are tossed on board of them at the last moment. Friends are bidding farewell! Wives tremble and look pale. There is a tear in the stout-hearted sailor's eye as he waves his adieu. But, " Give way, give way there, my lads; heave away my hearties!" The vessel clears the dock, passes through the gut, and then pauses for a brief space at the pier, while the sails are set and trimmed. Then comes the final word, " Cast off that rope!" and many a time have we, at hearing it, tugged with our tiny hands until we have succeeded in effecting it, and then strutted away as proudly as if we had just won Waterloo or Trafalgar. And now the sails fill; she moves, she starts, there is a cheer, " Off she goes!" dashing the spray on either side of her as soon as ever she feels the breeze. And now all the river is alive. The heavy Baltic vessels are creeping away. The Americans, always the same, are cracking along with every stitch of canvas they can carry. The West Indiamen sail nobly along, like the very rulers of the ocean. There are the coasters, and the Irish traders, and packets, while the smart pilot-boat dashes along under easy sail, here, there, and everywhere almost at the same time. And so they go on, until, like a dissolving view, they are lost behind the Rock, and we retire from our post, with the determination to be there again when the same scene is repeated.

CHAPTER II.

BUT the peace of which we spoke in our last chapter was nothing but a hollow and armed truce, which gave both parties time to breathe for a few months. England was suspicious. Napoleon was ambitious. The press galled him to the quick. At all events, "the dogs of war" were hardly tied up before they were again "let slip"; and then into what a bustle, and what a fever of excitement, do we remember old Liverpool to have been plunged. What cautions and precautions we used to take, both by land and water. We had a venerable guard ship in the river, the "Princess," which we believe had originally been a Dutch man-of-war, and, if built to swim, was certainly never intended to sail. There she used to lie at her moorings, opposite the old George's Dock pier, lazily swinging backwards and forwards, with the ebbing and flowing of the tide, and looking as if she had been built expressly for that very purpose and no other. Her very shadow seemed to grow into that part of the river on which she lay. But, besides her, we had generally some old-fashioned vessel of war, which had come round from Portsmouth or Plymouth to receive volunteers, or impressed men. A word about these last.   Those who live in these "piping times of peace" have no idea of the means which were employed in the days of which we are speaking, to man our vessels of war. The sailors in our merchant service had to run the gauntlet, as it were, for their liberty, from one end of the world to the other. A ship of war, falling in with a merchant vessel in any part of the globe, would unceremoniously take from her the best seamen, leaving her just hands enough to bring her home. As they approached the English shore, our cruisers, hovering in all directions, would take their pick of the remainder. But the great terror of the sailor was the press gang. Such was the dread in which this force was held by the blue-jackets, that they would often take to their boats on the other side of the Black Rock, that they might conceal themselves in Cheshire; and many a vessel had to be brought into port by a lot of riggers and carpenters, sent round by the owner for that purpose. And, truly, according to our reminiscences, the press-gang was, even to look at, something calculated to strike fear into a stout man's heart. They had what they called a "Rendezvous," in different parts of the town. There was one we recollect, in Old Strand-street. From the upper window there was always a flag flying, to notify to volunteers what sort of businsss was transacted there. But look at the door, and at the people who are issuing from it. They are the Press-gang. At their head there was generally a rakish, dissipated, but determined looking officer, in a very seedy uniform and shabby hat. And what followers! Fierce, savage, stern, villainous-looking fellows were they, as ready to cut a throat as eat their breakfast. What an uproar their appearance always made in the streets! The men scowled at them as they passed; the women openly scoffed at them; the children screamed, and hid themselves behind doors or fled round the corners. And how rapidly the word was passed from mouth to mouth, that there were "hawks abroad," so as to give time to any poor sailor who had incautiously ventured from his place of concealment to return to it. But woe unto him if there were no warning voice to tell him of the coming danger; he was seized upon as if he were a common felon, deprived of his liberty, torn from his home, his friends, his parents, wife or children, hurried to the rendezvous-house, examined, passed, and sent on board the tender, like a negro to a slave ship. And so it went on, until the floating prison was filled with captives, when the living cargo was sent round to one of the outports, and the prisoners were divided among the vessels of war which were in want of men. Persons of the present generation have certainly heard of the press-gang, but they never attempt to realise the horrors by which it was accompanied. Nay, the generality seem to us to hardly believe in its existence, but rather to classify it with *Gulliver's Travels, Don Quixote, Robinson Crusoe,* or the *Heathen Mythology*. But we can recollect its working. We have seen the strong man bent to tears, and reduced to woman's weakness by it. We have seen parents made, as it were, childless, through its operation; the wife widowed, with a husband yet alive; children orphaned by the forcible abduction of their fathers. And yet, there were many in those days, not only naval men, but statesmen and legislators, who venerated the press-gang as one of the pillars and institutions of the country. In those days, indeed! We much fear that, if even now we could look into the heart of hearts of many a veteran admiral and captain, we should find that they have, in the event of a war, no other plan in their heads for manning the navy but a return to this dreadful and oppressive system. We would, however, recommend those in whose department it lies to be devising some other scheme, as we are strongly impressed with the conviction that public opinion will not in these days tolerate, under any plea or excuse of necessity, such an infringement upon the liberty of the subject. But we are not writing a political article, but only describing our old-world fashions. Pretty rows and riots, you may suppose, now and then occurred betwen the press-gang and the fighting part of the public; and not a few do we remember to have witnessed in our younger days. On more than one occasion we have seen a rendezvous-house gutted and levelled to the ground.

Sometimes the sailors and their friends would show fight, and, as the mob always joined them, the press-gang invariably got the worst of it in such battles. Sometimes, too, the press-gangers would "get into the wrong box," and "take the wrong sow by the ear," by seizing an American sailor or a carpenter, and then there was sure to be a squall. The bells from the shipbuilding yards would boom out their warning call in the latter case, and thousands would muster to set their companion at liberty. A press-gangman was occasionally tarred and feathered in those days, when caught alone. We remember, as if it were only yesterday, walking down South Castle Street (it was Pool Lane then), with the Old Dock, where the Custom-house now stands, before us. It was, for some reason or other, tolerably clear of ships at the time. We well remember, however, that there was one large vessel, or hulk, somewhere about the middle. Before we tell what happened, we must observe that, attached to the Strand Street press-gang, there was one most extra piratical-looking scoundrel, named Jack Something-or-other. Perhaps, as is often the case, "they gave the devil more than his due;" but, if one half of the things said against this Jack were true, he deserved to be far and away prince and potentate and prime minister in Madame Tussaud's Chamber of Horrors. Well, as aforesaid, the Old Dock was in front of us, when all at once we heard a noise behind us, which told us that the game was up, and the hounds well laid on and in full cry.

At the same moment, Jack shot past us, like an arrow from a bow, while hundreds of men, women, and children, were howling, shouting, screaming, yelling, threatening close behind him. Every street sent forth its crowd to intercept him. There was no turning until he reached the dock-quay, but there the carters and porters rushed forward to stop him. What was to be done? How was he to escape?

The dock, as we said before, was in front, and there was the vessel in the middle. Without a moment's hesitation, the terrified wretch took the water, dived, like Rob Roy, to baffle his pursuers, and soon gained the deck of the hulk. Some talked of boarding her, and dragging him from his concealment; but the majority of the mob decided that justice was better than vengeance, and, satisfied with Jack's fright and ducking, concluded that although he was a bad one, he was game, and would make them more sport another time, and so dispersed.

CHAPTER III.

E spoke of the old guardship, the "Princess," in our last chapter. Many and many a time have we walked on her deck, until we thought that we ourselves might grow into a Nelson, a St. Vincent, or a Collingwood. Her captain, who used to take us on board with him, in the days of which we speak, was Colquitt — Captain Colquitt, of course, when afloat, but, on shore, among his friends, and he had many, Sam Colquitt, glorious Sam, pleasant Sam, clever Sam, up to anything, equal to anything, with a never-failing amount of fun and frolic, and an untiring fund of conversation, generally instructive, always agreeable, a giver and taker of a joke, full of anecdote, and the best teller of a good story we ever met with. We like to dwell upon his name. Much of the happiness of our boyhood sprung from our acquaintance with him. Beyond him, we recollect but the name of one of the crowd of faces which we used to see in the "Princess," the purser's clerk, named Vardy, a tall, fine looking fellow, some six feet two in height. And where are all the rest of them? How many survive? And where, and how, are those who do, supported?

Besides the "Princess," and the tubs of tenders which came round for the impressed men, we had occasionally a livelier and more interesting kind of craft in the Mersey. A dashing sloop of war would now and then look in, after a cruise in the Channel, and occasionally would act as convoy to any fleet of vessels bent upon a long voyage. It was interesting to see the start of one of these accumulations of ships, under the care of their watchful guardian. There they lay in the river, all prepared to make sail whenever she made the signal, with all sorts of noises and confusion going on among their crews. In the midst of them she was at anchor, with everything made snug on board, lying like a duck on the water, with silence and order prevailing from one end of her to the other. Spying glasses are turned towards her, but there is no appearance of hurry or anxiety. The wind chops round, and is favourable for outward-bound vessels. Still all is quiet and motionless in the man-of-war. We are not nautical, recollect, and only speak in landsman's phraseology. What we cannot accomplish we will not attempt. All eyes are now anxiously bent towards her, and the skippers of the merchantmen begin inwardly, and perhaps outwardly, some of them, to curse the caprice, or ignorance, or indolence of her captain; but, all in good time, gentlemen. Let him alone, if you please. He knows what he is about. He is only doubting whether the change of wind will hold. At last he is satisfied, and look!—a flash—a smoke—bang! It is the signal gun to make ready; another to weigh anchor—another to set sail—and away she goes, gracefully, like a hen followed by her chickens; or, to speak more appropriately, like a sheep-dog marshalling the flock. Sailing in convoy was certainly all equality and fraternity, but there was no liberty. The fast-sailing vessels were compelled to hoist no more canvass than would enable their slow companions to keep up with them. It was like the bed of Procrustes applied to sea affairs. And what fun it was to watch the crowd of vessels as they rounded the narrow channel by the Rock; such bumping and thumping, such fidgeting and signal-firing on the part of the guardian angel to check the fast ones, and stimulate the slow ones, and keep them all well together.

Nor must we forget here to mention another class of vessels, which made a very remarkable and prominent feature of the days which we are describing. We speak of the privateer. Liverpool was famous for this kind of craft. The fastest sailing vessels were, of course, selected for this service; and, as the men shipped on board of them were safe, in virtue of the letter of marque, from impressment, the most dashing and daring of the sailors came out of their hiding-holes to take service in them. On the day when such a vessel left the dock, the captain, or owner, generally gave a grand dinner to his friends, and it was a great treat to be of the party. While the good things were being discussed in the cabin, toasts given, speeches made, and all the rest of it, she continued to cruise in the river, with music playing, colours flying, the centre of attraction and admiration, " the observed of all observers," as she dashed like a flying-fish through the water. And then the crew? The captain was always some brave, daring man, who had fought his way to his position. The officers were selected for the same qualities; and the men—what a reckless, dreadnaught, dare-devil collection of human beings, half-disciplined, but yet ready to obey every order, the more desperate the better. Your true privateer's-man was a sort of "half-horse, half-aligator, with a streak of lightning" in his composition—something like a man-of-war's man, but much more like a pirate—generally with a superabundance of whisker, as if he held, with Samson, that his strength was in the quantity of his hair. And how they would cheer, and be cheered, as we passed any other vessel in the river; and when the eating and drinking and speaking and toasting were over, and the boat was lowered, and the guests were in it, how they would cheer again, more lustily than ever, as the rope was cast off, and, as the landsmen were got rid of, put about their own vessel, with fortune and the world before them, and French West Indiamen and Spanish galleons in hope and prospect. Those were jolly days to some people, but we trust we may never see the like of them again. The dashing man-of-war, and the daring privateer, dazzled the eyes of the understanding, and kindled wild and fierce enthusiasm on all sides. The Park and Tower guns and the *Extraordinary Gazette* confirmed the madness, and kept up a constant fever of excitement. But count the cost. Lift up the veil, and peep at the hideous features of the demon of war. Look at the mouldering corruption beneath the whited sepulchre of glory! But no sermons, if you please.

And there were the old Dublin packets in those days, before steam had turned sailor. If you took a passage in one of them, and had a fair wind, and were lucky, you might hope to arrive in Dublin some time, but if the wind were against you, then, as the old coachman said of the railway smash, " Where were you ? " You would be heard of eventually, when worn to a skeleton, and in a fit of indigestion from eating your shoe soles in the agony of starvation. And some of us used to get an annual voyage to Hilbre Island, an exploit which set us up as sailors for life. Occasionally visitors penetrated about as often to the one good house which was near the magazines. The Old Priory at Birkenhead was then " alone in its glory." All Cheshire, indeed, was in those days a kind of Africa, inviting and daring the young Bruces and Mungo Parks of Liverpool to explore it. We considered it to abound in deserts and Great Saharas. To penetrate to Wallasey, or to Upton, was to reach Timbuctoo. Bidston and the Lighthouse were our Cairo and the Pyramids; and as to Leasowe Castle, we cared not to approach it, under especial guardianship of so many fairies, ghosts, and hobgoblins was it supposed to be. These things sound like so many fables at the present day, when our steamboats, bridging the river, carry us across by thousands every hour. But in those times, an occasional ferry-boat was the only communication between the Lancashire and Cheshire shores of the Mersey. Few loved to cross from the one to the other, except under the pressure of business or necessity. Many persons, indeed, going from Liverpool to Chester, would travel round by Warrington, rather than chance a rough passage across the river in a small dangerous-looking boat. But *nous avons changé tout cela*. The things which we have been telling only live in the memory of a very few old fellows like ourselves.

CHAPTER IV.

BUT when the war, at the beginning of the century, was renewed with Napoleon, the preparations against him were not confined to the water. We had not only our guardship in the river, but the town itself was stoutly garrisoned against any enemy. We had always several regiments of regular soldiers or militia quartered here. But, besides these, O! what drumming and fifing and bugling and trumpeting there used to be among the regiments of our own raising; for old Liverpool did her duty well and nobly in those days of threatened invasion. Young and old, gentle and simple, high and lowly were all alike seized with a military fever and a patriotic glow, and hastened to don red coats and cocked hats, carry muskets, or wear swords by their sides. And some famous soldiers we had amongst us, and plenty of them. Let us see. There was Colonel Bolton's regiment, consisting of as fine and well-disciplined a body of men as ever mounted guard in St. James's or Buckingham Palace. In what awe we used to stand of the tall, upright, somewhat prim, and starched old colonel, as, mounted on his favourite white charger, he marched, band

playing, colours flying, at the head of his men, round
and round Mosslake fields, looking, both he and they,
defiance at all the world in general, and Napoleon,
and Ney, and Soult, and Lannes, and Davoust, and
Murat, and all the rest of the frog-eaters in particular.
And then there was the fine old major, called Joe
Greaves among his familiars, who lived at the top of
Mount Pleasant, and kept a glorious house, and welcomed everybody, and was welcome everywhere. A
fine fellow was the major as ever we set eyes upon,
and he was the father of as fine a family as ever
sprung up, like olive branches, round any man's table.
He was always kind, affable, and good-natured,
whenever we met him. Peace to his memory! And
Sir Thomas Brancker, quiet citizen as he now looks,
used to wear, to us, a most formidable aspect, when
an officer in Bolton's Invincibles. Occasionally he
would act as adjutant to the regiment, and, if our
memory does not fail us at this distance of time, we
once saw him—we certainly saw some one achieve the
feat—ride at a troublesome boy, who would intrude
within the line of sentinels, and leap his horse clear
over the head of the terrified urchin. We also recollect a Hurry and an Aspinall, officers in this regiment.
There was also Colonel Williams's regiment of volunteers, a fine body of men, and well ordered and
officered. The colonel had seen some hard service,
and heard real hostile bullets whistling abroad. He
was a strict disciplinarian, and a good soldier. We
need not attempt to describe him. He lived to so ripe
an old age, and to the last took such an active part in

our public affairs, that most of our readers must have his picture, in his white Russian ducks, fully impressed upon their memory. He was an ardent lover of his race and of his country, spared no labour in the cause of improvement and reform, and in earnestness, and sincerity, and integrity of purpose never was surpassed. Moreover, we had Colonel Earle's regiment of Fusiliers; a company of Artillery, commanded by Major Brancker, the father of Sir Thomas; a Customhouse Corps; a Rifle Corps, second to none in the country; and Major Faulkner's Light Horse, better mounted than any cavalry in the service. And the military infection spread so far that the very boys at the schools used to form themselves into regiments, and drum about the streets, with their little colours streaming in their front. And what reviews there were on the North Shore, and sham fights! And the waterside carts were all numbered, so as to be easily brought into use in case of an enemy appearing. Occasionally the soldiers were practised in them. Benches for seats were placed in them, and they would drive off as if for some distant place, to which a railway would now carry them like a flash of lightning. Once or twice there were sham alarms, raised in the night to try the activity and spirit of our volunteers; and O! what rattling of artillery, galloping of horsemen, beating of drums, and blowing of trumpets aroused the affrighted women and children from their beds, to look at the crowds of soldiers rushing through the streets to the several places of mustering for which they were bound. One of the most distinguished officers quartered amongst us in those bustling old times was Colonel Stuart, now the Marquis of Londonderry. A strange man is this said old marquis reported to be, and funny stories are told of him as ambassador at Vienna, and in various matters, political and diplomatic. But, nevertheless, a daring and gallant soldier was he in his youth; and, as a cavalry officer, in dash and skill, was reckoned, not only second, but almost equal, to Murat, the Marquis of Anglesea, and perhaps Jerome Buonaparte, whose desperate charges at Waterloo drew from his brother the exclamation, that if all had fought like him the day would have had a different issue. Well do we recollect Colonel Stuart, on his prancing Arabian horse, which he had brought with him from the Egyptian campaign; and a noble pair they looked as they dashed along. There was a rumour at the time, let us hope an idle one, that this steed of Araby was begged from him by a royal duke, and subsequently passed into a hackney coach. And how well do we recollect the encampment which was formed one summer, somewhere towards Litherland, and how the proud soldiers, living under tents, fancied that they were undergoing all the horrors and hardships of war in behalf of their beloved country. And what heroes we had in command of this military district. There was old General Benson, whose quarters were in Islington, a little of a martinet, and more of a prig, with a large slice of the pedant in things warlike—a regular old pig-tail, but reputed to be a good soldier. After him, we had a hero of another cut, figure, and appearance, General Fisher, whom it was glorious to behold. We will attempt to describe him. It was his custom to creep up Duke Street, where he was quartered, every morning before breakfast. He used to have on a pair of long, light blue pantaloons; slippers, down at the heels; a seedy coat, dear at three-halfpence for a scare-crow; a cocked hat to match, with much more grease than nap on it—we all hated Nap in those days—and a little feather, about two inches high, just peeping above it. And then the figure of fun arrayed in these habiliments. The general was a stout man, with rather a protuberant corporation. His cheeks bore the marks, it may be of many campaigns, but certainly of many vintages. He blushed port wine unceasingly. His nose, no small one, grew into something like a large bulbous root towards the extremity; and he wore a pig-tail, huge in its dimensions, both as to length, breadth, and thickness, even in those days of pig-tails. Such was the one-time champion of this district, as he might be seen creeping every morning through the streets, with his hands in his pantaloon pockets, not unlike an old pantaloon himself, and with a crowd of little boys admiring the war-like apparition, but strongly doubting whether it was St. George or the Dragon that stood before them.

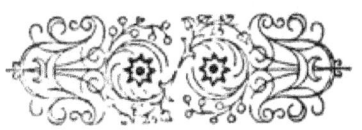

CHAPTER V.

WE spoke, in our last chapter, of the false alarms by which the soldiers forming our garrison were once or twice called together in the night, to try their zeal and alacrity; and we said how terribly alarmed were the women and children on such occasions. But we can, as truly as proudly, add that their fears did not extend to our brave and gallant volunteers. They rushed to their gathering spots, wild and eager for the coming danger, and, we verily believe, were sorely disappointed when they found that the actual opportunity had not arrived for teaching the enemy how Englishmen could fight for their country, their king, their altars, hearths, and homes. Let us, however, be thankful that we were never subjected to the horrors of invasion, but that the bold front of our champions kept it and them at a distance. The worst of our military fever was, that, in imitation of the bad practice of real soldiers at that day, it led to several duels. One of them ended fatally, a member of one of the most respectable families in the town having fallen by the hand of another, with whom he had always previously been on the most intimate terms. It was supposed at the time that this sad affair was encouraged by some who should have made every exertion and used every effort to have prevented it, but did not.

We have already spoken of several of the general officers who commanded in this district at the time we speak of. There was one, however, who will occupy a larger space in our canvas than we can afford to give to any other. When our military enthusiasm was at its height, Prince William Frederick of Gloucester came down to take the command. It has always been said that "Liverpool loves a lord," and there is some truth in the sarcasm. You may fancy, then, into what a fever of loyalty we were all thrown, young as well as old, by the presence of a prince of the blood royal amongst us, the veritable nephew of "the good old king," George the Third. And then how that fever grew and inflamed into actual white heat when the Duke of Gloucester, the king's brother and the father of the prince, arrived on a visit to his son. We remember him as if it were but yesterday; a fine, benevolent-looking old man, who was all smiles and kindness as he spoke to you. The prince himself was a tall, handsome, noble-looking young man, not too clever, as some of his intimates whispered, as they profanely called him " Silly Billy," the name having been originally fastened upon him by his royal cousin, subsequently George the Fourth, of splendid and dissipated memory. But what of that? We did not want him to set the Mersey on fire, but to fight if fighting were to become necessary. And O! what gaieties, what parties, what festivities, what flirtations, we had in honour of his arrival and residence amongst us. Beauty was beauty in those days, and so the prince thought, and so did the train of gallant and glorious staff-officers who accompanied him. There was the magnificent Mrs. ——, and the pretty Mrs. ——, and the clever Mrs. ——, and the splendid-looking Miss ——. How other hearts beat, perhaps with jealousy, perhaps with spite, as the prince, at most of the gay parties, generally devoted himself, more or less, to one or other of these Lancashire witches. Occasionally, however, a fit of formality came over him, and then nothing could be so stupid as to have the honour of meeting him. The duke, his father, had not married a bit of German silver, but had followed the bent of his inclinations and united himself to an English lady of great beauty. This led to the passing of the Royal Marriage Act. To annoy the prince, under these circumstances, his cousins used to raise a question occasionally whether he should be called Highness or Royal Highness, although there was no doubt that the latter was his title. This made him ever and anon tenacious of the amount of honour and respect to be paid to him, and when the fit was upon him, he would push etiquette to the extreme, and keep the whole company standing in his presence, just as another prince does sometimes at the present day. But when he did relax, he could be a delightful companion. He possessed prodigious strength, and was very fond of displaying it at those times when he forgot his stiffness and starch. There was, however, one sad interruption to the worship and adoration with which he had hitherto been surrounded in Liverpool. The Prince of Wales (George the Fourth) and the Duke of Clarence (the sailor king) paid a visit to "the good old town." As the stars twinkle not before the moon, and the moon herself pales before the brighter beams of the sun, so certain of our tuft-hunters here forgot the respect which was due and which they had long paid to the prince, in their anxiety to bow down and render homage to the new and passing visitors. We are not going to recount all the follies of the occasion. How the Duke of Clarence pushed a milk-pail from a poor girl's head, in Water-street, and then astonished her with a guinea for her loss, and so forth. We shall hasten at once to a scene which took place at the Town Hall. A magnificent banquet was given there by the Mayor of the time being. The Prince of Wales, the Duke of Clarence, Prince William Frederick of Gloucester, the Earls of Derby and Sefton, with a crowd of military officers, were present. After dinner the usual toasts were proposed; then the Prince of Wales and the Duke of Clarence, each with three times three. At last it was Prince William's turn, when, under the influence of some demon of mischief, the Mayor, instead of proposing his health, as usual, with all his titles and all the honours, foolishly consulted the Prince of Wales and the Duke of Clarence on the subject, asking in what form he should give the toast, and whether he should say Highness or Royal Highness. The answer of the Prince of Wales was said to be, " Certainly not Royal Highness, and without the honours," while the

Duke of Clarence more bluntly replied, "D—— him, don't give him at all." The Mayor then rose and simply proposed, "The commander-in-chief of the District, Prince William Frederick of Gloucester." It was drunk in solemn silence. The company all looked grave, as feeling that, under the influence of a higher idolatry, a gross insult had been offered to the late god of Liverpool adoration. Fierce glances were exchanged between the staff-officers and the other military men present. The prince himself writhed under the stroke, like a wounded tiger smarting under the lance of the hunter. Fire and brimstone and the devil himself flashed from his eyes, but he kept his seat. Presently the fearful and appalling silence was broken by the voice of the Mayor, calling out, as the next toast, "The lord-lieutenant of the county, with three times three," the three times three omitted at the name of the commander-in-chief, being revived with that of the next toast. A thunderbolt falling into the midst of the party could not have caused more astonishment and excitement. There could be no mistake now. The insult was meant to be an insult, and nothing but an open, prominent, and most insulting insult. The words had hardly passed from the lips of the Mayor, when Prince William, glancing a signal to his staff, who had their eyes fixed upon him, rose from his seat and left the room, followed not only by them, but by the whole of the military officers of his command who were present, leaving the table almost deserted, the Mayor gaping in amazement, and the royal cousins astounded at the spirit which they had evoked, more, perhaps, in mischief than in wanton insolence. However that may have been, from that day forth there was an uncomfortable feeling between the people of Liverpool and Prince William. It is only just to the rest of the corporation and to the gentry of the place to state, that to a man they felt strongly that an unwarrantable insult had been offered to him. He was, we believe, persuaded of this, but he never could be cordial again. If he forgave, he could not forget, the slight and mortification to which he had been so publicly exposed.

CHAPTER VI.

WE have already said that, in the days of which we are speaking, the Cheshire side of the Mersey, now bridged to us by steam, was a *terra incognita* to the general inhabitants of Liverpool. Almost as little was known of Aigburth, Childwall, Knotty Ash, Walton, West Derby, and so forth. Our fashionables were then satisfied to live in their comfortable town residences, without looking upon a country house and garden, and hothouse, as necessary to their existence. And we question whether they were not as happy as, we are certain they were more sociable and hospitable than, their more refined and degenerate children. We had not so many sets, cliques, and coteries. Men were more sincere than flashy in those times, and their entertainments more solid than showy. But we must not omit to give a "local habitation and a name" to some of our old leaders. The Hollinsheads lived then, and for many a day after, in the big family house near the canal. Some few respectable families lingered in Oldhall-street, to which the venerable Mrs. Linacre, who lived through so many generations, stuck to the last. Mr. Drinkwater, the father of Sir

George, inhabited a large house in Water-street. Jonas Bold lived splendidly at the lower end of Redcross-street. The market at that period was held round St. George's church, and chiefly in the space then contracted by a row of houses standing between it and the Crescent, in the rear of which stood a narrow, winding street, called Castle Ditch, communicating with Lord-street, then very narrow, and with no pretentions to attract admiration or even notice from the casual passenger, although the shops in it were always among the best in the town. In Church-street lived the old and respectable family of the Cases, now represented by Mr. J. D. Case, formerly a member of our town council, and at present a resident in Cheshire. His father, George Case, was for many years the leader of the Tory party in the ancient town council, and was, without exception, the best chairman of a public meeting whom we ever met with. Clayton-square was a strong resort of our leading and substantial merchants. Many a happy day have we spent in what was then the splendid mansion of the Rodie family. Kind, magnificent, and munificent in their hospitalities, but now, alas, without a representative of even the name surviving. Dr. Currie, so celebrated in his day, and so celebrated yet, lived in Basnett-street.

Bold-street had its Tobins, Aspinalls, Dawsons, &c. That kind-hearted man, Rector Renshaw, lived here in a corner house, with its door opening upon Newington-bridge. A little farther, on the opposite side, was the house of the famous John Foster, the most influential, as he assuredly was the cleverest, man of his day; the father of the generation who have lived and died amongst us, abused, every one of them, for their name, but admitted, all and each, to have been gifted men in their several callings and professions. Opposite to the house of Rector Renshaw was that of Harry Park, as we familiarly called him, the Abernethy or Astley Cooper of Liverpool; as a surgeon, we believe, second to no man of his day. At the very next door lived Dr. Brandreth, of whose eminence, or pre-eminence, as a physician, it is impossible to speak too highly. In all our wanderings over, and sojournings in, different parts of the world, we never remember to have met with a medical man whose standing was so thoroughly ascertained, admitted, and appreciated. And his position was as elevated in the social as in the medical world. There was no appeal against the fiats which Fashion issued from her seat in Bold-street. We now come to Slater-street, then only partially built upon. Here lived the Myers family, and here resided Mr. Tobin—at a much later period, Sir John.

In Seel-street was Mr. Perry, the first dentist of his day and locality; and next door to him lived the tremendous Mrs. Oates, the best instructress of small children in the rudiments of English whom the world has ever seen. She had the knack of measuring baby capacity, and of drawing out all that it contained, helped thereto, doubtless, by a concentrated essence of birch-rod-look which she constantly wore in school-hours, and which had "no mistake" written upon it in large letters. At all events, her name was celebrated at that day in all our public schools, as the best grounder and trainer of the young idea from whom they ever received recruits. But now we are in Duke-street, one of the most fashionable streets in the town at that remote period, and for some years afterwards. Here lived Mr. Whitehouse, and Mr. Peter Ellames. A little higher up resided a glorious old soul, Mr., afterwards Sir William Barton, as hearty a true Briton as ever walked on shoe-leather, and who had many experiences to tell of the West Indies in general, and Barbadoes in particular; and many also were the jokes tossed off at his expense. There used to be a nigger song quoted against him, extemporised by the black poets, it was said, on some occasion when he had lost a horse-race in Barbadoes. Some of the jingling rhymes we recollect ran thus:

"Massa Barton, Massa Barton, we are sorry for your loss;
But when you run again you must get a better oss!"

And then, as they rushed away at his supposed angry approach, came—

"Run boys, run, run for your life,
For here comes Massa Barton with his stick and knife."

At a later period, when Sir William was mayor, a very laughable occurrence took place at his own table. A gentleman, rising to propose his worship's health, thus commenced his speech, "Addressing myself to you, sir," &c., but it so happened that Sir William, who was no enemy to a jolly full bottle, or two if you like, was, by this time, in a tolerably muddy, misty, and oblivious state of mind, having no tangible recollections at the moment, save and except of his Barbadian experiences, where "you sir" was the term of contempt used by the master to the slave. Up jumped his worship, his eyes sparkling with wine and wrath, and with much hiccuping, exclaimed, "You sir, you sir, good heavens, you sir, that I should have lived to be called you sir!" Then down he bumped, looking like Mars, Bacchus, Apollo, rolled all into one, but continuing to start up and interjectionally to shout, "You sir!" until he fell asleep and slipped under the table. Nobody, however, laughed more heartily the next morning at the scene than did the mayor himself, who had returned from Barbadoes to Duke-street.

A few doors from Barton lived John Bridge Aspinall, a man much esteemed by all in his day, princely in his hospitalities, and with a heart and hand open to every call of charity. Then came Leather, Naylor, Black, Penkett, and a crowd of solid and substantial men, much looked up to and regarded at that time. But whose noble mansion have we here? Built by one of the Lake family, it was subsequently, for many years, the residence of a townsman whose name was identified with Liverpool, and who, comparatively speaking, but lately departed from amongst us. We talk of John Bolton, a man who worked his own way up from poverty to riches, and then lived in the most magnificent way, and in so becoming a manner that he might have been born to the magnificence in which he lived. No one knew the value of silence better than

Mr. Bolton. He had not received much education, but he saved appearances by making it an invariable rule never to open his mouth on a subject he did not understand. But we must stop to-day in the catalogue of our worthies. It may sound to some of our young readers like a dry chronicle of names. But never mind them. There are still some old stagers, like ourselves, left, and they will be delighted with this flight back to the men and things of their youthful days. Like veterans, we still love the clash of arms, and to fight our battles over again; and we much mistake if Liverpool were not at least as remarkable then for its guiding and leading spirits as it is now.

CHAPTER VII.

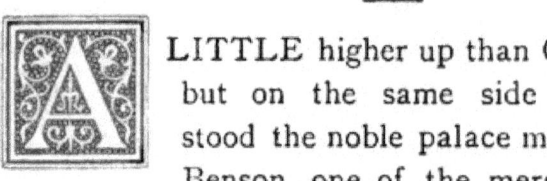 LITTLE higher up than Colonel Bolton's, but on the same side of Duke-street, stood the noble palace mansion of Moses Benson, one of the merchant princes of the old times of which we are speaking, with its gardens and pleasure grounds, bounded on one side by Cornwallis-street, and on the other by Kent-street, and extending backwards to St. James-street. In Duke-street also lived his son, Ralph Benson, one of the pleasantest and most agreeable men we ever met with, but somewhat, indeed, too much of a Lothario. After his father's death he resided at Lutwyche, in Shropshire, became connected with the turf, and represented Stafford in several parliaments. His wife, Mrs. Ralph Benson, was an Irish lady, of good family,—a Ross Lewin, we believe,—a charming person, handsome, and accomplished, who gave delightful parties, where all the wits and fashionables of the day used to assemble. And here we must say that the beaux of those times were beaux indeed. There are none such to be met with at the Wellington-rooms now, or seen at the windows of the Palatine Club. The Littledales, Hamiltons, Duncans, Dawsons, Lakes, etc., of that

generation,—where are they now?—were then a list of fine young fellows. And all the parties were so set off by the red jackets and blue jackets of our brave defenders, who made strange havoc among the ladies' hearts. Among the staff-officers who figured at them all, how well we remember the names and faces of Moultrie, Cox, Oisted, Higgins, and a host of others. And let us not forget the naval aid-de-camp of the Duke of Gloucester, Captain Browne, whose fine manly bearing and noble person must still be impressed upon the memories of many of our older readers. He was a true specimen of the British sailor, deeply respected by all who knew him, as well by landsmen as in naval circles. A generation later, if we may take such a jump, we had, among the staff-officers quartered here, Bainbrigge, now a general, and one of the ablest officers in the service, and one of the cleverest men out of it. There was Peddie, also, a delightful man among those with whom he was intimate. Nor must we forget William, we should say Major William, Brackenbury, a charming fellow, as the ladies said, and a rattling, pleasant, agreeable companion, as all admitted, the life and charm of every party, equal to a good song, and foremost in the dance. But what miracles does time work! Major Brackenbury, and his charger, and his dashing uniform, and his waving plume left Liverpool, and we lost sight of him for a long season. Years elapsed, when we went on a visit to a friend, who lived in a remote village in a far-off corner of the country. One day two strangers were announced. They were a deputation from some missionary society, and had come to invite our host to attend a meeting to be held that evening at the village schoolroom. They were grave looking persons; hair combed down, black coats, white ties, and all the rest of it. As they entered, we were sure that we had seen the countenance of one of them before. We looked at him, and he looked at us. The recognition was mutual, and at the same instant. "By Jove, Brackenbury," said we. "Ah, —— !" exclaimed he, not less warmly, but less profanely; and in an instant, after a hearty hand-shaking, we went back at rattling railway pace to the old times, the old people, and the old memories, to the bewilderment of both of our friends, but clearly to the utter horror of his grave companion. But we could not stop till we had it all out, nor till then could we proceed to business. He died soon afterwards. Poor fellow! he was a good soldier in his soldier days. And his closing career was that of a good Christian. Peace to his memory! And when we go, may those who survive us be able to say the same of us.

But to return to our story. In Duke-street, from which he subsequently removed to Walton Hall, at that time likewise lived Thomas Leyland, the eminent banker, who, from small beginnings, worked his way, by energy, industry, and perseverance, to the possession of immense wealth. He was a man of amazing shrewdness, sagacity, and prudence. When the north countryman was asked for the receipt of his ale, which was always good, he answered, "There's just a way of doing it, man." And so it was with Mr. Leyland. He had "just the way of doing things." We will not compare him to the animals which are said "to see the wind," but, by some intuition, instinct, or presentiment, call it what you will, he seemed always to have a warning of any coming storm in the money market, and trimmed and steered the ship, and took in sail accordingly. He was a fine-looking man, with what some thought a stern and forbidding, but what we should call a firm and decided look. We remember him with favour and gratitude. We received many civilities, and not a few substantial kindnesses, from him in his day. We omitted to state that what is now the Waterloo hotel,* at the bottom of Ranelagh-street, was then the mansion of the Staniforth family. The son, Samuel, lived to be an old man amongst us, and was once the mayor of Liverpool, and afterwards sunk down into being the stamp distributor of the district. He was a gentlemanly kind of person in society, but of a strangely austere and forbidding aspect, the most vinegar-visaged man we ever beheld. And the index was a correct representative of the inner man. When the election poet wrote of him "Sulky Sam Staniforth," he drew his character in those three words. By his marriage with a most estimable lady, he was closely connected with the Case, Littledale, and Bolton families. His son came in for the great bulk of Colonel Bolton's wealth, to the exclusion of his own relations; one of the happily rare instances in which a north countryman forgets his own blood in the disposal of his property.

* Since removed, with other premises, for the Central Station.

We now approach Colquitt-street, in which resided that shrewd, plodding merchant, Gilbert Henderson, the father of our respected and able Recorder. Here, also, lived Thomas Parr, who afterwards retired into Shropshire. His house was disposed of by a tontine, and, at a later day, became the Royal Institution, from which so many youths have gone forth to encounter the storms or pluck the honours of the world. Here, likewise, lived that true-hearted man of the old school, Peter Whitfield Brancker, one of the worthiest among the worthies of the days we write of. He was one who eschewed anything like nonsense, and was highly gifted with common sense. What he said he meant, and what he did he did with all his heart and soul. Few thought that he had so much kindness beneath his somewhat blunt and bluff bearing; and many called him selfish, when he laid up for his family what others threw away upon vanity and ostentation. We always looked upon him as one of the best men of the day; and, although he was a silent man in general company, he was far before most of our merchant princes in reading and intellectual attainments. In Rodney-street, then only partially built upon, lived Mr. Leicester, and also that "fine old English gentleman," Pudsey Dawson, who was the delight of our boyhood, as we listened to his powers of talking, and watched, with amazement, his capabilities for taking snuff. He was the father of, we may say, besides his other sons, a race of heroes. William, who was in the Royal Navy, distinguished himself greatly in the East Indies, by the capture, after a desperate action, of a French frigate, which had long been an annoyance and a thorn in the side of our trade in that quarter. Another fell, gloriously, in Spain. Charles, a lamb in society, a lion in battle, was killed at Waterloo. If our memory holds good, both of these last mentioned were then in the 52nd, a crack regiment in the famous fighting brigade of those gunpowder times. Noble old Pudsey Dawson! How he would talk by the hour, of wars and rumours of wars, to the circle which would gather round him at the Athenæum, until, as he turned from one to another, the whole ring in which he moved might be tracked by the overflow of his snuff-box. And what a horror he had of Napoleon and Frenchmen and everything French. It was well for them, as he used to say, that he was not at Blucher's elbow when he entered Paris, it being his firm belief that the earth would never be quiet, until that city of trouble and confusion was blotted from its face. But Liverpool society could not point to a man of whom it was prouder, or one more respected, esteemed, or honoured, than this same Pudsey Dawson. All men liked him, and we did not make an exception.

CHAPTER VIII.

IN Rodney-street, likewise, lived Fletcher Raincock, one of the most remarkable characters of his day. He had few equals in a legal capacity, and no superiors in literary attainments. He had a most gluttonous appetite for books, and read everything, old and new. He was a regular "curiosity shop" in the variety of his knowledge, and could produce all sorts of odds and ends at a moment's notice, from all sorts of ancient authors, unknown to and never heard of by other people. This made him a most agreeable companion, his conversational powers being tremendous, and set off, rather than impaired, by a spice of originality and eccentricity, just enough to draw a line between him and the common herd of ordinary and every-day people by whom he was surrounded. Like Yorick, "he would set the table in a roar," by the combined wit and wisdom which he had ever at command. And while speaking of lawyers, let us digress for a moment to mention another old giant of those times. We allude to Mr. Hargreaves, who was for some years the Recorder of Liverpool, a deep and profound lawyer, *haud ulli veterum virtute secundus*. He was succeeded by James Clarke, who lived to a much later date amongst us. Poor Clarke! We never thought him crushed down by the weight of legal lore which he carried. But he was a man given to books, and had learned much from them. A pleasant man in a party, too, he was, abounding in anecdote and the passing stories of the day. And, on one point, we must admit that he was unmatched. We never met with any one who possessed more shrewdness and knowledge of the world. He had thoroughly studied the volume of man as well as printed books, and we often point to his career as a proof of the usefulness of this knowledge. He had a remarkable coolness and calmness about his character, but we did once see him put into a regular "fix," in his own court, by an obstreperous juryman, who would have a will of his own. A huge sailor and a small boy were being tried for stealing an immense piece of cable. The sailor threw it all upon the boy, and the Recorder, believing him, was charging the jury to the same effect, when one of them rising, and hitching up his trousers, commenced, "But, Mr. Recorder!" This was too much. Mr. Recorder, electrified with indignation at being so interrupted, looked his best thunderbolts at the remonstrant, who still, however, kept sturdily on his legs, muttering protests against the opinion of the bench. The spectators became excited and amused at such an unusual scene, and a titter went round the court. This only added fuel to the fire, and Mr. Recorder made another attempt to silence his persevering assailant. "I tell you," he exclaimed, "that from the evidence, the boy must have been the culprit who carried off the cable;

the law says so, and I say so." But the obdurate juryman had not yet done. He instantly answered, "But, Mr. Recorder, I do not know what you and the law may tell me, but common sense tells me that that boy could not even lift that piece of cable from the ground, much less run away with it." This was a poser with a vengeance. It was a new and original view of the case, which set all evidence at naught. The titter in the court grew into a regular burst of laughter, which nothing could check. The poor Recorder was fully nonplussed and nonsuited, and the jury acquitted the boy without a moment's hesitation.

And here, if we may descend from barristers to solicitors, let us render a tribute of respect to the memory of a fine old fellow, a practitioner in the latter branch of the legal profession. We speak of George Rowe, of whom we knew much, and nothing but what was admirable. He was a warm friend and a delightful companion. He loved the good things of this world, but he liked others to enjoy them with him. He was fond of society, and in his own house kept, we always thought, the best table in Liverpool. But we we were going to speak of him as a lawyer. We cannot fathom the exact depth of his reading in Coke, Blackstone, and so forth. We leave his head, to speak of his heart. And in this point of view, we can mention several things which will prove that, unless lawyers in general are greatly maligned, George Rowe was a miracle of a lawyer, in allowing the milk of human kindness to flow so largely through his nature. We recollect an instance in which he offended and lost an old and valuable client, because he refused to make a will for him which he thought unjust towards the gentleman's own family and relations. And more instances than one could we tell of in which he worked, and included even expensive papers, documents, and stamps, all "free gratis for nothing," for poor and deserving parties who had solicited his help in the expectation that they were to pay for it on the usual terms. There may be others in the profession, and we trust there are many, equally liberal and kind-hearted. But knowing it of him, we tell it, and we add further, that, in our voyage of life, we never met a kinder, a warmer, and a truer friend. We honoured him in life, and in death we treasure his name and memory.

In Queen-square lived another family, called, with a different spelling, Roe, and of most respectable standing were they, among the substantial old stagers of the town. In the same locality resided Colonel Graham, and also another party upon whom we must bestow a somewhat longer notice. This was Mr. John Shaw, commonly called Jack Shaw, a man of immense wealth and intense vulgarity. Never was there such a sacrifice to the golden calf as that betrayed, not simply by the elevation of such a person to the highest municipal honours, and the civic chair, but in giving him an influence which he held undisturbed for years. He was positively known by the *sobriquet* of "the King of the Council," or "King Jack." His grammar was truly *à la* Malaprop. On one occasion we recollect hearing him, when wishing to be fine, call the old constables his "mermaids," instead of his "myrmidons." At another time, when he was sitting on the bench, the Town-clerk observed to him that a sentence which he was about to pass would be contrary to the Act of Parliament, when the magisterial despot silenced his functionary by retorting, "D—— your Acts of Parliament. What cares I for your Acts of Parliament?" He had a habit also of invariably pronouncing the word "digest" as if it were "disgust." One day, at his own table, he had a waggish friend of his, Carruthers, dining with him. The fish was not very good, as Jack always dealt in the cheapest market. Carruthers rather turned up his nose at the savour, but his host fell to with the greatest vigour, observing, "Oh, I can disgust anything." "Yes, by ——, that you can," exclaimed C., with a roaring laugh. Presently, however, Jack paid him off, as he thought, with compound interest. "Carruthers, my boy, how many shirts a week do you wear?" said he. "One every day, and sometimes more," was the answer. "Why, man," was Jack's rejoinder, "what a dirty hide you must have. One serves me a fortnight." Such were the municipal pleasantries of the municipal monarch of his day. We believe that it was the same worthy potentate who once threatened to "*slat* an inkstand at the head of a Jew, who was a witness before him, if he did not tell him what his Christian name was," and he would have said the same thing to a Turk or a Hindoo.

We believe it was the same Jack who once complained to the late Egerton Smith that he had not reported something that he had said fairly, when that respected editor facetiously replied, that "if he ever grumbled again, he would report everything he uttered on the bench or elsewhere, *verbatim et literatim*, exactly as he delivered it." But our readers must not suppose that because, by some strange metamorphosis more wonderful than any related by Ovid, this awful Jack was translated into a Town-Councilman, we had, therefore, a whole council of such men. Far from it. Jack was a pelican in the wilderness, a thing out of place, an accidental nuisance, how and why admitted into that body, it is impossible now even to guess. As a whole, and with this exception, the old Town Council of Liverpool consisted of some of the first and most respectable and most respected men in the place. Its fault was, that it was too exclusive; like the late Whig cabinet, too much of a family affair. It did its work well in its day; we may, indeed, say remarkably well, considering its irresponsibility. But a change was demanded with the changing times. We sometimes question, however, whether we have improved the class of men. Then it was selection, without election; now it is too often election, without selection. But the present system has this great advantage: a black sheep is not a perpetuity. We can get rid of him at the end of his three years, and that is something, and a great something.

CHAPTER IX.

IN Mount Pleasant lived, in those good old times, Sir George Dunbar, the representative of an ancient race in Scotland, and a model gentleman, both in appearance and manners. He was originally in business in Liverpool; but when the family title descended to him, the pride of ancestry was stronger than the pride of "the merchant prince" within him, and he retired from vulgar trade, cut sugar hogsheads and rum puncheons, and was no more seen on the "Rialto," discussing markets and inquiring the price of barilla and pearl ashes. It was a false move on the part of the worthy baronet. No rank would have been sullied by remaining in the firm of which he was the head. His junior partners, Ewart and Rutson, became not only eminent, but pre-eminent, amongst our giants of that day, and achieved a name and reputation known to the ends of the earth, and are still well represented amongst us. The son of the latter is a large landowner in Yorkshire, universally respected; while, of the family of the former, one son, William, has long been in parliament, and another, Joseph Christopher, was a candidate for

Liverpool at a recent general election. But the Dunbars have altogether vanished from the scene. The best of them that we knew, poor Tom Dunbar, was one of the handsomest and cleverest, and certainly the most brilliant and the wittiest, of mankind. He had abilities for anything, for everything, but he never cultivated them; at all events, he never used them. He wanted either application or resolution. It might be the pride of his father in another shape. He was a lounger where he might have been a leader. He was satisfied to flash and dazzle as a meteor in society, while men much less intellectually endowed, but of a more persevering and plodding spirit, passed over him, and became persons of mark, position, and distinction. It was mortifying to his friends to see him ever with the game in his hands, yet always throwing up the cards. His active life amounted to just *nil;* but his sayings, his polished witticisms, his delightful retorts, his splendid and pungent repartees, in English, Greek, and Latin, would fill volumes. They are still treasured by the survivors of the circle of which he was the life and joy and pride, and brought out every now and then, with a sadly smiling countenance, as one of Dunbar's gems: just as on high and grand days we go to the oldest bin for a bottle of the best vintage. And everything was original with him. He never borrowed nor repeated. It was fresh and fresh with him, as often as you met him.

But we must pass on. Russell-street and Clarence-street had no existence in those days. In St. Anne-

Street resided the old families of Bridge, Fisher, and Rogers. Here also lived Mr. Blundell, the clergyman; Mr. Smith, at a later period of Fulwood Lodge; and Mr. Haywood, the father of the eminent cotton-broker of that name. Close to St. Anne's Church was the house of a celebrated character amongst us, both then and long afterwards. We speak of Mr. Thomas Wilson, profanely called Tommy Wilson, the dancing-master, by his wicked pupils. A good fellow was Tommy, although a strict disciplinarian in "teaching the young idea," not "how to shoot," but how to turn out its toes and go through the positions. But, unfortunately, Mr. Wilson grew too ambitious, and, instead of contenting himself with fiddling for boys and girls to dance to, would preside over orchestras and concerts, and cater for the amusement of the public, by which we fear he did not grow too rich. He was a worthy, warm-hearted man in his way, and somewhat of an original, and withal possessing the good opinion of all who knew him. Nor must we forget to state that in St. Anne-street likewise lived Mr. Rutson, of whom we have already spoken. His partner, Mr. Ewart, resided in Birchfield. In Soho-street was the house of Mr. Butler, somewhat too convivial in his habits, but one of the most thorough gentlemen we ever met with. His son is the present Mr. Butler Cole, of Cote and Kirkland Halls, both in this county. In Rose-place, then a fashionable suburb, more country than town, resided Mr. Lake, who subsequently retired to Birkenhead Priory, and afterwards to Castle Godwyn, in Gloucestershire. He was the father of the Captain Lake whose wound from a Minié rifle, at Weedon, was recently mentioned in the newspapers. A little further out towards the green fields, now all streets, we come to the mansion of a noble old worthy of those times, Edward Houghton, the father of Richard and Raymond, of "that ilk," so well known and so much respected amongst us. How well we remember his amiable and benevolent countenance! He had a kind word for everybody, and was prompt to do kind acts too. And what a staunch sportsman he was, seldom missing his bird, and devoted to his work. And then what a famous breed of pointers he had, jet black and all black. How they would set and back set. How they would range the stubble and never flush a partridge nor run a hare. How they would "down charge" at the sound of a gun, without a word being said. We wonder whether any of the descendants of this celebrated race of dogs are yet in being.

But, before we pass beyond the boundaries of the old borough, let us hark back a little, and enumerate a few more of the ancient worthies, or "standards," of the town whom we have omitted in the foregoing catalogue. There were the Boardman, Harding, Bancroft, Downward, and Lorimer families. Nor must we forget to mention that admiration of our boyhood, William Peatt Litt. He always seemed to us to be the original of the lines—

> "Old King Cole was a jolly old soul,
> And a jolly old soul was he."

A munificent, magnificent, generous, hospitable soul indeed was Mr. Litt. There are few like him now. And there were several families of the Byroms. The Naylors and Bournes, the grandfathers of the present generation of those names, lived in Duke-street, and were among the most respectable and respected of our citizens. There, also, lived Mr. Patrick Black, a fine old stager even at the time we speak of. We can see him yet before us. Picture to yourselves a kind and venerable man, in a cloak enveloping his whole body from head to foot, a gold-headed cane in his hand, and a wig. Oh! such a wig, a regular wig of wigs, as white as the whitest of hair-powder could make it, of a transcendental cauliflower appearance, and in size far beyond the proportions of the largest Sunday wig assigned to Dr. Johnson in the pictures which have come down to us. We recollect once, when about some six years old, getting into an awful scrape about this said venerable gentleman and his megatherium wig. We were walking with a small friend of our own age and inches, when suddenly the apparition of Mr. Patrick Black, arrayed as we have described him, came in sight. Our admiration, as usual, burst forth in the far from respectful and almost profane exclamation, "There goes old Black with his white wig." Hardly were the words out of our mouth, when a gentle tap came upon our shoulders, and a soft whisper fell upon our ear, " Master ——, if it would be any particular pleasure to you, I will ask my father to wear a black wig in future." We looked round, and, O! horror of horrors! were we not thrown into real agonies, and almost hysterics, when, in the person uttering this mild remonstrance, we recognised the daughter of the old gentleman whose wig we had been blaspheming? We stammered and hammered at an excuse, and then ran for our life. And for many a long day we disappeared round the nearest corner as quickly as possible if any of the Black family came in sight of us in our walks. The joke, however, got wind, and it was long before our martyrdom and persecution ceased, even in our own circle, where "Old Black with his white wig" was thrown into our teeth whenever we were inclined to be obstreperous and naughty. Neither must we forget the name of Brian Smith, who lived in Bold-street, and whose very look was a picture of benevolence. John Leigh, too, the attorney, a man of gravity and silence, but with a very intelligent countenance, lived then in Basnett-street. As we shall have occasion to mention his name in a future chapter, we shall merely allude to it here. And there was the firm of M'Iver, M'Viccar, and M'Corquodale, never mentioned by us youngsters without the addition of the awfully bad joke about the old woman, a mythological old woman doubtless, going into their office and asking if they were the house of M'Viper, M'Adder, and M'Crocodile.

But who is this "Goliath of Gath" whom we see approaching, and whom, if he had lived in these days and been a poor man, Barnum would certainly have bagged, and caravaned, and made a fortune out of as a giant? It is Roger Leigh, as kind-hearted a man as ever lived, with an amiable and benevolent smile ever playing upon and irradiating his huge countenance. He was a general favourite, as he walked amongst us like Gulliver among the Liliputians. And what a character he was at an election! His activity and energy in such times were tremendous. But Roger was rather a paradox in his politics. A Roman Catholic in his religion, he was what was then called "a Church and King man" to the backbone; a Tory of Tories, in days when Tories were not the faint-hearted chickens which we now see them. Poor old Roger Leigh! Like Sir Abel Handy, he had always some scheme on the anvil for getting rich, but we fear that, like the rest of us, he sometimes took two steps backward for one forward. The stone of Sisyphus is the type of most of us. But, rich or poor, successful or otherwise, peace to his memory! We never heard harm of him. He had everybody's good word. We wish that the world contained many more like him.

CHAPTER X.

HE who undertakes to be the chronicler of Liverpool society at the commencement, and in the early years, of the present century, must not forget to mention the old and respectable families of Gildart and Golightly. And who is this easy, good-tempered soul, whom the mind's eye now brings before us? It is Mr. William Rigg, profanely called "Billy Rigg" by his familiars. And who comes next? Henry Clay, frank, jovial, light-hearted fellow, once Mayor of Liverpool, and a generous and hospitable chief magistrate he made. And there goes that veritable ancient, Arthur Onslow, collector of customs, with a name which testifies that family interest was as strong in those days as it is in these. And now, if we go on 'Change, surely this is an original whom we see before us. His name is Brown, but among the gentlemen "on the flags" he is better known as "Muckle John," A shrewd, sagacious man of business is he, as ever lived; and many were the stories which used to be told of his sayings and doings and somewhat sharp practice in his money transactions. "Mr. So-and-so will be my security to you," said some gentleman one day to him.

"Aye, mon, but who will be the security for the security?" was his retort. In after life we became acquainted with the celebrated "Jemmy Woods," the Gloucester banker, and it always struck us that he strongly resembled "Muckle John" in many features of his character, especially in *crescit amor nummi quantum ipsa pecunia crescit*. The cash book seemed to be father and mother, wife and child, comfort and consolation, joy and glory of both of them. But we had reached Great Nelson-street North before we turned back again into the town. A little further on, in Everton, lived Mr. Thomas Hinde, second to none here in his day. The representatives of his family are now to be found at Lancaster. At Everton, likewise, resided Mr. Shaw, the father of Mr. Thomas Shaw; also one of the Earle family; another brother lived then, and long afterwards, at Spekelands. At St. Domingo was the mansion of Mr. Sparling. The country-houses beyond that were "few and far between." Close to the old London-road, about two miles from Liverpool, lived Mr. Falkner, the Major of the Liverpool Light Horse. A mile or two further out was Oak-hill, the seat of Mr. Joseph Leigh, one of the most pushing and rich of our enterprising merchants, and as fine, handsome looking a fellow as you may meet with in a ten days' journey. The march of intellect did not advance per railway in those times; and Mr. Leigh, although marvellously at home in arithmetic, compound addition, the rule of three, multiplication and so forth, had not much studied history, poetics, and the other graces, and, as by many they were then thought, exotics of education. Consequently endless were the stories told of his blunders and mistakes in the literary line when he crept up in life, and thought it necessary to come out as a Mæcenas. For instance, it was said that, in ordering his library, he directed that so many feet of books should be placed in it, and that, when asked if he would have them bound in Russia, he answered promptly, "No, in England, to be sure!" On one occasion, a waggish bookseller asserted that he called at his shop and told him that, as Shakespeare was considered to be such a first-rate writer, he must send him immediately any more works which he might publish; while on another, after surveying shelf after shelf covered with books having Tom. for Vol. inscribed upon their backs, he exclaimed, in the highest degree of admiration, "Upon my word, that Tom must have been a monstrous clever fellow." We, of course, receive such accounts *cum grano salis*, or to speak in more mercantile phrase, with a little discount, not as absolutely fabulous, but as somewhat highly coloured. Moreover, we have no doubt that, in addition to his own blunders, Mr. Leigh was made to bear all "the tales of our grandfathers" in previous circulation. He subsequently removed to Belmont, a splendid place in Cheshire, when the proud squires of that proud county took up the ball, and coined and circulated all sorts of odd tales about him. In their visits, one with another, they passed from house to house for a week at least, and brought with them an immense retinue of horses and servants. And it was a standing joke for years among them, that, when first

Mr. Leigh settled in that part of the country, he told some of them who called upon him that he should be happy to see them at tea occasionally. But as we have also heard this story told against the first Mr. France, of Bostock Hall, who also passed from Liverpool into Cheshire, it may not have been originally levelled against Mr. Leigh. Another laugh, however, against him was, that some village wag, who probably had not been valued at his own price by some of the new inmates of Belmont, inscribed over the lodge gates, where they were found one morning, the following doggrel:—

"In this house there is no beer,
In this park there are no deer.
And why? Joe Leigh lives here."

We must, however, recollect that the Cheshire squires had then, and probably have yet, a strong aversion to Liverpool and all its works. Looking at their mortgages,—for in those days a Cheshire squire without mortgages would have been a *rara avis* indeed,—they had a sort of prophetic feeling that the merchant princes of Liverpool were destined to eat them up, like another Canaan; in other words, to buy the acres of all the wiseacres in the county, and so exterminate the original squirearchy. *Hinc illæ lachrymæ.* Hence, when they lost the game, they took their revenge in bad jokes which kill nobody, and, indeed, are very harmless affairs, if, as the French proverb has it, *Il rit bien qui rit le dernier*, he has the best of the laugh who has the last of it. Mr. Leigh had a brother, a very quiet and respectable man. He lived in Duke-street at one time, and afterwards at Roby Hall.

But, in speaking of Everton just now, we forgot to mention William Harper, one of the wealthiest men of his day, a blunt, downright sort of person, a member of the old corporation, and mayor in his turn. He also had made an encroachment on the pride, and trod on the toes, of the Cheshire squires, by buying an estate at Davenham, near Northwich. He had three daughters, co-heiresses, whom, when at school, he never forgot to toast at his own table as "The lasses of Ashbourn." Some people thought this a good joke, and it was even alluded to in some of the election squibs of the day. But we always admired the old man for it, and looked upon it as an excellent trait in his character. One of them married Mr. Hoskins, or, as he afterwards became, Mr. Hoskins Harper. Another was Mrs. Formby. The third was united to Dr. Brandreth, or, as he was called in his father's lifetime, Dr. Joseph Brandreth, who, in the second generation, has so well maintained the medical distinction achieved by the first.

But to return from this digression; not far from Oak-hill was Highfield, now the seat of that prince of good fellows, Thomas Littledale, Esq., the chief magistrate of Liverpool, but then belonging to, and the residence of, the Parke family. A fine, glorious, jovial old man do we recollect Mr. Parke. He had three sons, whom we remember; Mr. Thomas Parke, Major Parke, and a third, of world-wide fame and celebrity,

Baron Parke, of whom "the gude old town" cannot be too proud, as first and foremost among the legal ornaments of the judicial bench.

Not far from Highfield was Ashfield House, the mansion of John Clarke, a brother of the Recorder, and himself a member of the Town Council, and once Mayor of Liverpool. He was a peculiarly good-looking little man, always well-dressed, rode a good horse, and drove a neat carriage. Further on we arrived at Broad Green, belonging to the Staniforth family. Mr. Ashton, whose sons and descendants still reside in the neighbourhood, lived at Woolton, honoured and respected by all the circle of his friends and acquaintance. At Childwall was the noble mansion of the Gascoignes, which has now passed into the hands of the Marquis of Salisbury, who married the only daughter and heiress of the last possessor, Bamber Gascoigne, who was at one time, as his ancestors had been before him, the member for Liverpool. His retired habits, however, and his literary tastes, interfered with his bringing any very great portion of activity to his duties, and on one occasion, having thereby been brought into collision with some of the merchant-princes amongst his constituents, they renounced their allegiance to him, but still, not altogether repudiating the family name, they selected as his successor his younger brother, the famous General Gascoigne, who, however, was a very inferior person to Bamber. But we shall come to him presently. At Childwall likewise resided Thomas Clarke, whose two brothers we have already mentioned; a man whose good-nature, generosity, and nobleness of soul have seldom been equalled, never surpassed. Mr. Clarke had also a splendid place, Peplow Hall, in Shropshire, now, we rather think, belonging to Lord Hill.

CHAPTER XI.

LIVERPOOL society, like that of every other place, has always been divided into sets; how formed, by what mysterious line separated into divisions and subdivisions, and sections, and cliques and coteries, we can no more tell than we can explain the causes at work to produce the eddies of the tide. There they are, and we must take them as we find them. It is so, always was so, and ever will be so. But, in enumerating the old stagers of half-a-century ago, more or less, we have passed them in review " promiscuously, as it were," without undertaking the invidious task of cataloguing the particular set to which they individually belonged. Generally speaking, however, they may be placed under three heads: the fashionable set, the wealthy and commercial set, and the Corporation set. But many of those who have been named belonged to all of these sets. There was, moreover, a literary set; but it was numerically very small. Its three principal ornaments were Dr. Currie, Dr. Shepherd and Mr. Roscoe. The latter, who became so world famous at once, and so deservedly, was a remarkable and striking instance of the proverbially small estimation in which prophets are generally held in their own country. It is true that, by a momentary enthusiasm, he was sent to parliament to represent his native town. But it was transient and evanescent, and as speedily burnt out as a fire of stubble. Liverpool never appreciated Roscoe as the rest of the world appreciated him, nor does it now appreciate him as the rest of the world appreciates him, in spite of its feeble talk about his immortal memory, and its weak and mocking attempts to support Roscoe clubs. In any other place, his name would have been what Shakespeare's is to Stratford, "a household word," familiar in the mouth of age, manhood and childhood. But it is not so here, and with him. He has a small and decreasing circle of friends, who remember him when alive, and still treasure every word of wisdom which they ever heard from his lips. He has a somewhat wider circle of admirers, who read his works, and find a giant's hand impressed upon them all. And there are others who profess to read and admire, because they have learned that no badge of ignorance would be thought greater in the literary world than a confession that they have not studied the writings of Roscoe.

But when all these are counted, we still remain convinced that the general public of Liverpool, beginning from the topmost pinnacle of its society, possess a marvellously small knowledge, and as small an appreciation, of the literary remains of this illustrious man. We can give a remarkable instance of this, of which probably the generality of our readers have never heard. Not many years ago, a Liverpool lady, whose literary attainments are of the highest order, was, when in London, asked to meet a very select party combining some of the most intellectual, as well as the most aristocratic, persons of the west end of the metropolis. She was delighted with the company, and they were equally delighted with her, with her stores of information, her lively conversation, her brilliant wit, her sparkling repartee, the *tout ensemble* which made her the lion, or, speaking of a lady, the star of the day. But at last, unhappily for the moment, the name of Roscoe was mentioned, and she became astonished, confused, and silent as she heard him spoken of with an awe, an admiration, and a reverence due and paid only to minds of the most magnificent calibre. "Take any shape but that," she might have said, "and I can talk with the best here present." On this topic, however, she was mute, and her perplexity and annoyance were dreadfully increased when, at every pause, the rest of the party seemed to wait for her opinions and sentiments. "He was a Lancashire man. He was a Liverpool man. She must have visited, as the Mahommedan does his Mecca, with the steps of a pilgrim, every locality hallowed and consecrated by his presence and footsteps. She must have treasured and embalmed in her memory anecdotes of his sayings and doings which had not yet appeared in print; stories of his habits, and customs, and daily life, which enthusiasm had cherished and tradition handed down." But they laboured under a huge delusion. She was no Boswell, to read from her diary the hourly records of the life of another Dr. Johnson. In fact, she was ignorant on this point, and knew nothing of the man of whom they were speaking.

It may be explained. She was of an ultra-Tory family, with large estates in the West Indies, of which past generations had run passenger ships for involuntary black emigrants from Africa to the other side of the Atlantic. In her home circle, then, as a child, a girl, she had always heard Roscoe spoken of, not as a great philanthropist, not as a first-rate scholar, not as a writer whose books will be read and referred to until the world's last blaze, but as a busybody, as a meddler, as a mischief-monger, whose wish and object were to injure and destroy the town and trade of Liverpool. We may not wonder then that her amazement was great, and her perplexity not less, when now, for the first time in her life, she heard what was the public estimation in which her world-celebrated and world-appreciated townsman was held. The mists of local prejudice were at once scattered from before her eyes. She honestly and candidly took refuge in a confession of the truth, and so dissipated the half sneer, half smile of wonder which was gathering on the lips of some of the company. We recollect the circumstance well, and were not more amused than pleased with the avidity with which the very next day our fair friend provided herself with everything written by or of Roscoe, and with the keenness of appetite with which she set to work to devour them as speedily as possible. He is now one of the *Dii Majores* in her intellectual Pantheon. But we also mentioned Dr. Shepherd, *clarum et venerabile nomen*, as one of the literary giants of our locality some years since. He was, indeed, and no mistake about it.

We have frequently in our time heard him compared by turns with Theodore Hook and Sidney Smith. But he was, in our opinion, infinitely superior to either of those luminaries in the Metropolitan world of wit; and, had he shone in the same sky, our belief is that their lesser rays would have paled before his greater brilliancy, as the stars go out and tapers grow dull and dim when the sun is up and dazzling us with his glory. Dr. Shepherd was a thorough and solid scholar; an advantage not possessed by either of his rivals. Hook's education was notoriously deficient. Smith had not accumulated equal stores of learning from his. Hook, when not running riot as a *roué*, a debauchee, mad with dissipation, and intoxicated with the flattery of the circle in which he moved, never soared to anything beyond the character of a first class Jack Pudding. His practical jokes were those of a boy blackguard. His jokes uttered were almost invariably of the coarsest kind, which derived a momentary zest and relish, not from their own intrinsic value, but from the political excitement which then prevailed, and which they were generally intended to subserve. Friendship has indeed sought, in more than one biography, to rescue him from such a character. But friendship would have been more friendly, so to speak, if it would have allowed him to be forgotten.

There is no advocate so eloquent as oblivion for some reputations. With Sidney Smith, again, it was "Figaro here, Figaro there, Figaro everywhere." His whole life was one long, enduring, universal jest.

He never seems to have been serious. In all his conversations, and most of his writings, puns and points, often not soaring to sparkling antithesis or dazzling epigram, beset you, like "man traps and spring guns," at every turn in the road, until you become weary and exhausted, Man cannot always be laughing. A perpetual joker must sometimes excite a yawn. But we never found Dr. Shepherd guilty on this head, and in this fashion. He was witty in season, but not out of season. He could be the man of business. He could bring gravity to the discussion of grave affairs, and treat things serious with seriousness. But when in the social circle, and amongst his friends, it was the season for relaxing, then came forth the mighty stream of his wit, rolling like another Mississippi, in its glorious, resistless course, and sweeping all before it, and as remarkable for its point, polish and elegance, as for its strength and poignancy. There were few who could keep the saddle in the intellectual tournament with him. Before that terrible lance, adversary after adversary went down, like chaff before the wind. Nor do we recollect any greater treat than a perusal of the correspondence with which the Doctor used, from time to time, to season our newspaper reading. Upon whatever controversy he entered, he was sure to come off victorious. The very opposite to Mrs. Chick, whose maxim was to carry everything by "an effort," he never seemed to make any effort at all. It was the very ease with which he crushed the most daring of his foes which was so annoying to them, and so amusing to the spectators. How he would bowl down a whole string of sophistries, which had been boldly set up before the world as so many philosophical conclusions not to be overturned! How he would turn a fallacy inside out! How he would scatter every kind of mystification, and expose every attempt at falsehood and imposition! How he would strip every jackdaw of his borrowed plumes, and raise the laugh against every presuming quack! Yes! He was wit, scholar, philosopher, author, controversialist, all in one, and good in all. But he was something more. We believe Dr. Shepherd's charity, for his means, to have been something wonderful. We have heard of acts of kindness on his part which would have been pronounced noble had they been performed by the wealthiest of our merchant princes, or the highest in the land. What, then, were they, when done by one of his limited income and resources? His heart was a bank, upon which misery had only to draw, and its drafts were sure to be accepted and honoured. All respect to his name and memory! We know few men who have lived more esteemed; we know of none who have done more good in their time. Let his surviving friends join with us in offering this tribute to one of the giants of the past.

CHAPTER XII.

SOME people have very strange notions of the duties of the historian and the biographer. They fancy that our part is to suppress or distort the truth, and to substitute flattery for it; that we should deal in sickening and nauseous eulogy only,—

> "In sugar and spice,
> And all that's nice,"—

and exert our energies in the vain effort to extract sunbeams from cucumbers, or to make deal boards out of sawdust. The child, walking in the churchyard, and reading the epitaphs, exclaimed, "Mother, where do they bury the bad people, for I can only find the good ones here?" But we are not epitaph-mongers, we are not flattery-spinners, we are not eulogy-penners. We are not, we never were, a society of angels, and we take men as we find them. We are not making a collection of fancy sketches, to be all beauties. We are forming a cabinet of likenesses. We took up our pen with this end in view, and we shall continue to work it out. We shall tell "the

truth, the whole truth, and nothing but the truth."
We shall "nothing extenuate, and nought set down in
malice," but state facts as facts, call a spade a spade,
and describe men as they were, not as they ought to
have been. We have, of course, an object in these
prefatory remarks. We have. It seems that certain,
it may be well-intentioned, or it may be over squeam-
ish, censors and critics are bombarding us with good
advice, to the effect that we ought in chronicling the
past to praise everybody; in other words, as we have
already hinted, to write epitaphs, not history. But,
once for all, we beg leave to state that we are not
going to take this advice. We have, however, two
propositions to make in answer to it. The first is,
that those amiable persons who are shocked by our
plain speaking, should just skip our effusions; or, if
that does not satisfy them, we will surrender our task
and pen and inkstand altogether to them, and allow
them to begin with the next chapter, and carry our
work to a conclusion in their own fashion, which we
doubt not will be infinitely superior to our way of
putting our rough notes together, and stating our
homely thoughts in homely language. We trust that
this offer will be accepted. We would rather be
learners than teachers, and shall be delighted to be
convinced that every common councilman of the last
generation was a Chesterfield and an Adonis, and
every merchant a Lindley Murray and an Admirable
Crichton, miracles of wit, literature and learning.
But we, at all events, are not the Plutarch to record
the mythology, not the history, of these impossible

prodigies and inconceivable wonders. And now we proceed, until our critics volunteer to supersede us. But, verily, as we return to our work, *vires acquirit eundo*, it grows upon our hands. When first we undertook it, we had a notion that we could in a brace of chapters dot down all our reminiscences of the times we speak of. But here we are now, in Chapter XII, with as yet no port in view, and scudding along with all sail set over the interminable ocean of garrulity, and with our catalogue of worthies growing into a far greater magnitude than that of Homer's ships.

"Who goes there?" It is Mr. Birch, afterwards Sir Joseph, the father of our late worthy representative. A noble-looking specimen of the merchant prince and the "fine old English gentleman" was Mr. B., and much esteemed and respected by all who knew him. And look at the tall, commanding figure that now approaches. It is Mr. Brooks, the father of the venerable Rector and Archdeacon of that name. And there were the Walkers, who lived in Hanover-street, and who in their day were the very tip-top of the tip-tops, and the head of all the gaiety and fashion of Liverpool. And there were the Gregsons, ever one of our first and leading families; and the Heskeths, and the Midgleys, and the Caldwells. And Arthur Heywood, then a middle-aged man, has a foremost place in our recollections. And there were the Rathbones, Bensons and Croppers, of that generation, as brave-hearted and active and zealous philanthropists as their descendants of the present day. And there was Hugh Mulleneux, who went through a long life marked by deeds of charity, and who to the last of his life, was one of the most guileless and sterling men we ever met with. And there were the other families of the same name, with a different spelling, Thomas Molineux, William Molineux, and other brothers, of whom we can safely say that we never heard any evil, and knew much good. They had hearts exactly in the right place, and with the right feelings in them. They are worthily represented yet amongst us. Nor must we forget to chronicle the name of old Mr. Yates, whose sons still walk worthily in the steps of their respected sire. And there were Hughes and Duncan, and the celebrated world-famous "Tom Lowndes," who shot like a meteor across the sky of the commercial world, and who, in the magnificence of his speculations, would have thought no more of bidding for the United States for a cabbage garden, or of undertaking to pay off the national debt at a week's notice, than he would of swallowing his breakfast. A fine fellow comes next, Mr. Nicholson, or Colonel Nicholson, as we used to call him, a title which, we believe, he bore in the Militia. He was a gentleman, out and out, through and through, every inch of him, in look, in bearing, in manner, in feeling. We never saw, to our fancy, a handsomer man than he was in those days, and amiability sat on every feature of his noble countenance. And how he could skate! How we have by turns laughed, and trembled, and shouted, and clapped our young hands as we have watched him darting along on the St. Domingo pit, and then cutting figures of eight and all sorts of fancy forms and hieroglyphics on the ice, and taking the most surprising leaps, and achieving all kinds of dangerous miracles. But, *arma cedunt togæ*. The soldier subsequently subsided into the citizen. Mr. Nicholson became a member of the Corporation, and was Mayor of Liverpool. He married one of the Miss Roes, in Queen-square. She was a niece of the celebrated Council king, Mr. Shaw; and their son, having dropped his paternal name for that of his maternal great-uncle, now lives at Arrow, in Cheshire. He has a strong look of his father in his features, and seems to have inherited his kindness of heart and manner. And there go the Harveys, fine fellows every one of them. And there is noble old Rushton, who, like his son after him, our late respected and lamented magistrate, had a head upon his shoulders with something in it, and a heart swelling and flowing, aye, and overflowing, not merely with a river, but with an ocean, of "the milk of human kindness." Shall we ever "look upon his like again?" Selfishness was not in his nature. He felt for the woes and sorrows of his fellow-creatures, without respect to colour, climate, creed, or country. His sympathies were universal. The earth's limits alone were their limits. He might have taken for his motto the glorious sentiment which, nearly two thousand years ago, called forth such thunders of applause in the theatre of ancient Rome:

Homo sum, humani nil a me alienum puto.

All honour and respect and peace to his memory! But we must go on, although you may say—

"What! will the line stretch out to the crack of doom? Another yet?"

Yes; and one very different from our last-mentioned hero. The next figure upon our canvas was also a character in his way. Look at his bluff, resolute, determined countenance. It is Captain Crowe, as brave a sailor and as odd and eccentric a man as ever walked a quarter-deck. Once, in the good ship *Mary*, he fell in with two English sloops of war, somewhere in the middle passage, which Liverpool ships were engaged upon in those times. They took his trim-looking vessel for a French cruiser, and he took them for a couple of the same craft. It was, however, nothing to old Crowe that they were two to one. He was like the stout-hearted ancient, who said that he would count his enemies when he had beaten them. Night was coming on, and they could not distinguish each other's flags. To it they went, and kept at it hammer and tongs until morning showed them the English colours floating on all their masts. The cruisers had, in the dark, made several efforts to board him, and had been repulsed with terrible loss. The firing of course ceased as soon as the light showed them their mistake, and the senior commander of the man-of-war sent an officer on board, with a sulky civil message, to know if they could do anything for him in the way of helping him to repair damages. "I want nothing," said the old Turk, with a grim smile, which meant that he had given as much as he had taken in the action; "I want nothing, but a certificate to my owner that I have done my duty."

And who next? That is Taylor the brewer. And there is another of the same trade, jolly old Ackers, great in malt and hops, greater in politics, and greatest of all in the actual bustle and conflict of an election. And there is his friend with him, old Hesketh, the famous tailor, of Paradise-street. Instead of being the ninth part of a man, Hesketh was nine men all in one, the picture of a true Englishman, the very portrait of John Bull himself, a regular old Tory, for men, out of his trade, more than measures, and with such a good-tempered countenance, that it drew customers, better than a thousand advertisements, to his shop.

And there was another character who must not be excluded from the "curiosity shop" of our reminiscences. Every old stager must recollect Peter Tyrer, the coach-builder, and keeper of hackney coaches. A very primitive-looking man was old Peter, but as full of eccentricity and solemn jocularity as an egg is full of meat. Peter's jests were always uttered with a serious tone, and spoken out of his nose more than through his lips, so that we laughed at the twang when there was nothing else to laugh at. There was occasionally some originality in his humour; but he had one standing joke, a very grave one, which has now passed into a regular Joe Miller with the men of his craft. Whenever any one came to order the funeral cavalcade which he had to let out, he invariably pointed to the plumed hearse, of which he was very proud, and observed, " That is the very thing for you, for of all that have travelled by it none have ever been heard to complain that they had not an easy and pleasant journey by it." Poor Peter! And when thy turn came, we trust that thy journey, both to the grave and through it, was an easy one! Nor do we doubt it. With all his whims and oddities, Peter was a good man, no idle professor, but a zealous, practical Christian. We could do with more like him.

CHAPTER XIII.

AMONG the great West Indian merchants of the days we are writing of, we must not forget to place the James and France families. The representative of the latter resides at Bostock Hall, not far from Northwich, in Cheshire. The present Mr. James sat for some years in the House of Commons, and gave evidence of talent far beyond mediocrity. There was also a spice of originality about him which commanded attention whenever he spoke. It was but seldom, however, that he opened his lips. Senatorial honours, we presume, had no attractions for him. We so conclude from his voluntary and premature retreat from their pursuit, much to the regret of all his friends. There was another Mr. James in Liverpool in those days, rather a roughspun and unhewn kind of person, and very eccentric and amusing in his way, a character, in short, amongst his own circle. Many of our old readers must remember Gabriel James, or, "the Angel Gabriel," as some of his waggish friends called him. He had a ready tongue and plenty of mother wit, and seldom came off second best in a tilt and tournament with words. Nor must we omit to mention old

Mr. Waterhouse, of Everton, a grave and venerable-looking man, whom we always regarded with awe and reverence. There was Mr. Neilson, too, whose sons still uphold the family name amongst us with so much credit and respectability. And there was the lively, gay, agreeable "Jack Backhouse," who lived in Smithdown-lane; and Mr. Backhouse of Everton, and another family of the same name at Wavertree; and the Colquitts, and the Dawsons of Mossley-hill. And the gay parties in those times used frequently to be enlivened by Lord Henry Murray, who was often a visitor with the Neilsons and Backhouses.

And we had also our circle of wits, whose sharp sayings were passed round, as household words, from mouth to mouth, and so afforded pleasure and amusement, as they spread from set to set, from one extremity of society to the other. First and foremost in this bright and brilliant band, we must place Mr. Silvester Richmond, or "Sil Richmond," as he was generally called. Next to him was Joe Daltera. And with them we must join Sam Pole, and "Jim Gregson," who lived in Rodney-street, a man of racy humour, with a fund of originality about him which revelled in the utterance of good things. And here be it observed, that, as Liverpool is still called the town of "Dicky Sams," so, in those ancient days, its people were all Sils, and Joes, and Sams, and Jims. It was the custom of the place, and equally observable in every rank of society. But, for a time, let us speak of our prince of wits, Sil Richmond, who was one of the most sparkling, agreeable men ever met with in company. Amongst his own set no party was ever thought to be complete without him. He held the post of a searcher in the Customs, and many were the amusing stories, coined, perhaps, to raise a laugh at his expense, of the "diamond cut diamond" warfare carried on between him and persons striving to break the Revenue laws, of which he was a most vigilant guardian. His powers of conversation were immense, and never flagged. He was always the rocket, never the stick; and he was as potent with the pen as he was brilliant with the tongue. We may call him the poet laureate of the tories, with whom he warmly sided. The encounters, therefore, between him and Dr. Shepherd, who was ever the principal scribe for the liberal party, were frequent, fierce, and savage. His weapons were not quite so keen and polished as the doctor's, but they would do a great deal of mangling work, and, like Antæus springing from his mother earth, if foiled and thrown in one round, he was always ready for another. No amount of punishment could dishearten him, and he was always in wind, and, what is more, kept his temper unruffled in the thickest of the fray. He was the author of all the election squibs in his day. Out they poured, grave and gay, in prose and verse, and he seemed never to be exhausted. We doubt not that some of our old stagers yet retain many of them among their treasures and curiosities. One line in one of his songs is still as fresh upon our mind as if we had heard it but yesterday for the first time. Mr. Fogg, a butcher, was one of the most zealous and active canvassers in the reform ranks at some election. Richmond instantly had his eye upon him, and, bringing intellect as well as ink to the work, thus impaled him on the point of his wit as he spoke of him as

"A Fogg that could never be Mist."

This, of course, told better in the midst of political excitement; but still, at all times, we must admire it as a specimen of our friend's ready wit. We used often to look up at him in boyish wonder and admiration, as he cracked his jokes, and his filberts, and his bottle all at the same time. And one thing particularly struck us. He never led the laugh at his own jests, but looked as grave as a judge, and far more knowing, through his spectacles, while "setting the table in a roar." O, for another Hamlet! to say for us, "Alas, poor Yorick! I knew him well, Horatio; a fellow of infinite jest, of most excellent fancy," etc. Of Mr. Richmond's family, one went into the navy, and another into the army. They were both fine young fellows. The soldier, called after his father, distinguished himself and was wounded in the last, we hope that it will always be the last, American war.

But we spoke of Mr., *alias* "Joe," Daltera just now, as one of the circle of wits in the former days which are slipping from our memory. He was a regular character in his day and in his way. He was brought up to be a solicitor, and at one time was in partnership with the late Mr. Topham. He had abilities to have raised himself to the greatest eminence in his profession, but he wanted business habits. He had no application, no attention, no steadiness of purpose. In short, he was of a jovial, convivial turn of mind, full of fun and frolic and glee, was fond of company, and greatly preferred shining in society to poring over parchments. He was a terrible sitter at a party. He never sung, "We'll not go home till morning," but practically it was impossible to get rid of him until long after the short hours had set in; and, in truth, he was such a pleasant companion, so overflowing with sparkling conversation, "full of mirth and full of glee," as we said before, that no one ever made the attempt. Steady old fellows at whose houses he used to visit would say, before he arrived, "We will be rude to that Daltera to-night, and give him a hint that shall send him home in decent time." But when the appointed hour had struck, and long after, these same steady old boys, fascinated by Joe's wonderful powers of jest and anecdote, were the loudest in pressing him to keep his seat, a pressure which he never resisted. He thought, with Dibdin's famous song, that there was "nothing like grog," or, as he and his familiars called it, "rosin." Often, when you thought that at last he was really going, he would suddenly exclaim, instead of "one glass more," "Now, lads, rosin again, and then we'll positively go." He could not use his pen like Richmond, but he was quite his match in wit and repartee. Countless were the stories told of his sayings and doings. Once the watchman found him in the street quite unequal to steer his course home. This friend in need wished to place him in a wheelbarrow, and to carry him to his house in this kind of triumphal car, when Daltera, steadying himself for a moment, and throwing himself into a theatrical attitude, astonished "poor old Charley" as he addressed him, *a la* John Kemble, whom he had seen performing the character that night, "Villain, stand back; the gods take care of Cato!" We ourselves remember crossing the river with him, in one of the old-fashioned ferry-boats, before the invention of steamers. There was a stiff breeze, next door to a gale of wind, blowing, and we were in momentary peril from the rash attempt of the boatmen to head a ship at anchor. The sailors themselves were alarmed, while most of the passengers were in an agony of terror. One poor market-woman, in the excess of her fright, threw herself upon her knees in the middle of the boat, and burst out into the exclamation, "Lord have mercy upon us!" when the inveterate punster, alluding to the name of the river, thus cried out to her, "No, no, my good woman; do not say, 'The Lord have *Mersey* upon us' this time!" We were both vexed and shocked at the moment, as the jest out of season jarred upon our ears, while the crew and the passengers looked inclined to *extemporise* poor Joe into a Jonah at the instant. But we have often smiled at it since. Poor fellow, he could not help it. He could no more have kept it in than the effervescence will remain quiet in a ginger-beer bottle when the cork is drawn. It was the ruling passion strong in death, or in the face of death. Like Sheridan, "he had it in him, and it would come out." On another occasion, it was said that, upon landing from the boat at Runcorn, or some village between here and Chester, he was seized upon by several persons, who supposed him, from his dress of sober black, to be some celebrated preacher whom they expected, and were on the look out for. Joe, having made himself safe and certain on two points, namely, in the first place, that none of the villagers had ever seen the anticipated star; and, secondly, that he could not possibly arrive that day by any conveyance, humoured the mistake, was carried in triumph to the chapel, preached the most brilliant sermon ever heard, and delighted and won the hearts of the elders, by whom he was entertained, withal taking care to disappear from the scene the next morning before the real Simon Pure arrived. We do not, recollect, vouch for the accuracy of all the details connected with this episode. We only relate it as we have heard it related by Daltera himself a hundred times. Poor Joe! He had many friends and only one enemy, and that was himself. He wasted talents, energy, wit, brilliancy, which would have made an intellectual capital for a hundred shining characters. But who is faultless? Let us look at the beam in our own eye.

CHAPTER XIV.

IN our last chapter we mentioned the names of some of the wits and illustrious in jest of whom Liverpool could boast a few years since. We now descend the scale, to speak of a class whom we would mildly call "the practical jokers." The *Spectator* makes glorious old Sir Roger de Coverley horribly afraid of the club of Mohocks who, many years since, pushed their horse-play in the metropolis into positive ruffianism, and perpetrated the most savage outrages under the name of fun and frolic. But the sports of the Liverpool mischief-mongers at the commencement of the present century were of a much more harmless and innocent character. One young gentleman, who subsequently flourished as a grave old stager amongst us, had a passion for collecting, in a kind of museum, or "curiosity shop," all the signs and signboards which struck his fancy; and it was said that he had a large muster of black boys, carried off from the different tobacconists' shops in the town. And sometimes he varied the amusement in the following fashion:—In Pool-lane, now modernised into South Castle-street, was a famous ship-instrument maker's shop, in the front of which was elevated a wooden figure of a midshipman in full costume, at which we have often gazed with fond delight in ancient days, and which we are now convinced must have been the original of the one which Dickens, in Dombey, makes Captain Cuttle contemplate with so much pride and pleasure. Somewhere in the same locality was one of the tobacconists' shops of which we have spoken, with the then usual sign of a black boy over the door. Time after time would our funny and facetious friend substitute these signs one for the other, so that, when morning broke, the midshipman would shine forth in all his glory at the door of the snuff and tobacco store, while the black boy would be grinning in front of the ship-instrument maker's premises. At last the joke wore itself out. The perpetrator of it never was discovered. He preferred to play his "fantastic tricks" alone, and kept his own secret. But there were also associated bodies for the performance of the same kind of mad pranks. One set of them formed themselves into what they dignified with the name of "A Committee of Taste," although they and their friends called them, over their cups, "The Minions of the Moon." Their object seemed to be to emulate and imitate the merry doings of Falstaff and his companions. They occasionally, however, pushed their jokes somewhat too far. There was a house in Daulby-street, then a sort of *rus in urbe*, or, rather, country altogether. It had a garden in front, and was ornamented with a verandah. This it appears did not please these fastidious gentlemen, and the owner was served with a notice, signed by "the Chairman of the Committee of Taste," directing him to alter or remove it by a certain day. To this command he paid no attention. Well, the day arrived;

"'The ides of March are come.'
'Ay, Cæsar; but not gone.'"

The verandah was still there. But that very night, at a few minutes before twelve o'clock, a loud knock at the door called the owner of the house to the window which overlooked it. The moment he appeared, with his head and the nightcap upon it looming through the darkness, a cheer welcomed him from the opposite side of the street. Then came a pull, and smash, crash; the verandah, with all its trellis-work and ornaments, was gone. The rogues had sawed away the supports, made their ropes fast, and then, with wicked waggishness, summoned the gentleman of the house to witness the destruction of his offending property. We will chronicle another of the feats of the "Committee of Taste." At that period Mr. Samuel Staniforth lived in the large house at the bottom of Ranelagh-street, afterwards converted into the famous Waterloo Hotel. Something about it, either a shutter, or a knocker, or a bell-handle, we have forgotten which, was excommunicated by this tasteful inquisition, and ordered to be removed. Mr. Staniforth was about the last man in the world to obey such a lawless mandate, being one of that class who, "if reasons were as plentiful as blackberries, would not give one on compulsion." He therefore treated the notice served on him with contempt. And now the battle began in good earnest.

"When Greek meets Greek, then comes the tug of war."

the thing denounced, whatever it was, was removed, then restored, and again removed, to be once more restored, and still in the original offending form, without an atom of alteration. And so the struggle went on, until Mr. Staniforth became highly exasperated, as well as extremely indignant at the persevering annoyance. Of this, the jokers, who met him with grave and sympathising faces every day in society, were fully aware, and only made thereby more resolute in their fun. In the extremity of his vexation he consulted George Rowe, the attorney, of whom we have made honourable mention in a former chapter. We speak from authority, for we had the story from Mr. Rowe himself, who used often to tell it with great glee. When the offended alderman had unbosomed all his griefs to the solicitor, and had urged him to exert all his vigilance to discover the offenders, and then to put in force all the terrors and pains and penalties of the law against them, the latter met the history of his sorrows with one of his good-natured and hearty laughs, to the great astonishment of his client, who certainly did not belong to the laughing portion of the creation. When he had settled himself into seriousness, he said, "Well, Mr. Staniforth, I suppose, after all, your object is to abate the nuisance, rather than trounce the sinners." Staniforth, however, was not so sure that he would not like to do both, and "kill two birds with one stone." But at last, after a long and serious confabulation, he was persuaded to leave the whole affair in the hands of the lawyer, who, indeed, would only undertake it on that condition. Now Mr. Rowe, although he had no guilty knowledge of the offenders, had a shrewd guess in his own mind, and, acting upon the impulse, wrote a note, desiring to have a conference with the chief captain of the knocker and bell banditti. They met, and on the next day glorious old George, sending for Mr. Staniforth, laid the result before him. The latter was exceedingly angry at first when he heard that the bold rogues, instead of being overwhelmed with sorrow and remorse, still took up very high ground, being determined to make him capitulate on the immediate point at issue, but with a promise on their part that he should never more be annoyed by them on any other. At first he would listen to no such terms, regarding any treaty with the parties as little better than compounding for a felony. Gradually, however, he yielded to the reasonings of his adviser, and the agreement, without being duly signed and sealed, was honourably carried out on both sides. "And to whom," we said to George Rowe, when sitting one day with him after dinner, with our legs under his mahogany, "to whom did you address your note when you wanted to have this celebrated interview with the 'Chairman of the Committee of Taste?'" "Why, to Joe Daltera, to be sure," he answered, with a very thunder-clap of laughter, which almost made me tremble lest a blood vessel should burst or apoplexy ensue; "Why, to Joe Daltera, to be sure, who else could it be?"

But alas, alas! for the flight and power of time!

Of the actors in this amusing scene, all have passed from the arena of busy life. We marvel whether any of the aforesaid "Committee of Taste" yet survive, to sigh or to smile over the wild pranks of their youth! But how is it that such follies are only remembered, not perpetrated, now? As Mr. Pickwick observed, when prosecuted for a breach of promise, men are very much the victims and tools of circumstances. When we look at the class to which the parties of whom we have been speaking belonged, we can find many reasons, without any boast of merit and improvement, which will explain why young gentlemen in these times should not roam through the streets by night, bent upon fun and mischief, for hours and hours. Forty or fifty years ago, men met together to dine about three o'clock. They had, consequently, not only a longer time to devote to the bottle, but also, when they broke up, excited by wine, some hours to get through as best they could, before they retired to bed. This would have a wonderful influence upon their conduct. Moreover we had only a few old watchmen in those days, who were as much alarmed at the approach of our "bucks," as the travellers by an Eastern caravan at the appearance of the wild Arabs of the desert. Again, the introduction of gas for lighting the streets, instead of the old oil lamps which, "few and far between," used to twinkle in the distance and just to "make darkness visible," had a wonderful influence upon the habits of our young men. Some great authority on such matters in the metropolis calculated that, for enforcing order, one gas-lamp was equal, at least, to three policemen. There are many persons over whom the fear of being found out exerts a strong power. What they would do under the veil of darkness they strenuously avoid when its shelter is removed. The temptation may be strong, the will may be present, but the opportunity is wanting. These remarks, however, only apply to one class of society. But, when we make our survey more general, we must also take into account the march of knowledge, the increase of mechanics' and literary institutes, and the spread of cheap and useful books among the masses. To the printing-press we doubtless owe much for our improved tastes and habits. Who, indeed, can calculate the might, the magnitude, and extent of its diversified influences and powers? It is our schoolmaster, our instructor, our guide, our guardian, our police, all in one. Praise and honour to those who wield the pen, so long as they use it for the benefit and advantage of their fellow-creatures. Ill-disposed persons may pervert it to be an instrument of evil. But who can tell the amount of its well-doing when directed to good? Truly did the wit observe, that the greatest *stand* ever yet made for the improvement and civilisation of mankind was the *inkstand*.

CHAPTER XV.

 LITTLE back from Water-street, between it and St. Nicholas's Church, stood an ancient Tower in those days. It was one of the remaining antiquities of Liverpool. It had originally belonged to the Lathoms of Lathom, and subsequently passed, by the marriage of the heiress of that family, into the hands of the Stanleys, some generations before the elevation of that illustrious house to the Derby title. At a later period it had become an assembly-room, and, last of all, by one of those strange vicissitudes to which all earthly things are liable, was a prison for debtors. But at the time we speak of there it was, as if frowning in gloomy strength upon the encroachments which modern improvements and the spirit of enterprise were making on every side of it, a grim old giant, the type, and symbol, and representative of other times. As we contemplated its massive walls or walked under its shadow, what reflections it was calculated to awaken within us. We were then too young for our mind to dwell very seriously or very long upon such topics, but we have often since thought within ourselves that, if stone walls had ears, and eyes, and tongues, what

strange histories that old Tower could have told. It carried us back to what we call an age of romance, but what, in fact, was an age of stern and iron realities. What associations and recollections did the very sight of it conjure up within us! The monument of many centuries of glory and crime! In its day, although now merely an object of curiosity and a prison for debtors, the palace and fortress of nobles! In its day, perhaps, like other old castles within the land, the living grave, and the grave, when dead, of the guilty and innocent alike, of the ambitious and the victims of ambition, of heroes and saints, of martyrs and traitors, of princes and impostors, of patriots and conspirators! How often has the mailed chivalry of the middle ages rode forth through these gates in all its magnificence, pomp, and pride! How often has chained innocence been dragged through them to its dungeon's depths, and to the shambles to which, perchance, they were the passage, feeling, as they turned upon their grating hinges and shut it from the world for ever, all the tremendous force of the " Hope no more!" which the Italian poet wrote over the entrance to his Infernal Regions! If, we repeat, its walls had tongues, what wonders could they tell, what secrets reveal, what mysteries unravel! What mighty or memorable names have resided, or been imprisoned and perished here! What strange things have been enacted within these gray old stones now crumbling into ruin, while the wronged and the wrongdoers have together passed to judgment! But the period for indulging such contemplations has long since passed away. The spirit of feudalism, after holding its ground for so many centuries, at last yielded to the genius of commerce, and the gloomy old Tower was sacrificed upon the altars of modern improvement. Carters and porters now shout and swear where stout old knights and ladies fair held high revelry; and sugar hogsheads, and rum puncheons, and cotton bales are now hoisted, and roll, and creak, and clash where prisoners once groaned and chains clanked. It is a new version of *arma cedunt togæ*.

But we are becoming grave; we moralise; we preach; *Vive la bagatelle*. Let us go back for a few moments to the subject of the last chapter, and speak a little more of those mischief-mongers who dignified themselves with the title of " The Committee of Taste." We therein stated that Daltera was the understood or suspected head of the said Committee. On the same authority, neither better nor worse than the assertion of common report, it was whispered that, amongst its members, were some other dashing spirits of the day, to wit, Mr. William, *alias* " Billy Graham," " Young Sutton," as Mr. William of that ilk was always called, " Bob Pickering," *cum multis aliis*, the *multis aliis* including some, we find, who are yet amongst us, and whom, therefore, we would not name for all the world, and so expose them to their children and grandchildren, who look up to them as models of gravity, propriety, and piety. One venerable gentleman, whom, from his confessions, we suspect to have been at least an honorary member, said to us only the other day,—and in such a free and easy and impenitent sort of way, that we verily believe that, with youth restored, and opportunity returned, and policemen and gas-lamps extinguished, he would soon be at his old pranks again,—" Daltera was always preeminent for good taste, and was, therefore, elected President of the Committee." Finding that our friend was inclined to be communicative, we pressed him for more of his reminiscences, when he added, "They were fine fellows, and woe unto anything that came under their waggish displeasure!" They carried on, he told us, a long war, a repetition of that which has been already described between them and Mr. Staniforth, with Mr. Parke, the celebrated surgeon, touching the shape of his knocker. Dr. Solomon, who then lived in the large house at the top of Low-hill, had his grounds studded over with statues, of which he was not a little proud. They were voted to be not classical by the men of taste, and the decree went forth for their removal, and was carried out on the appointed night, when they were all taken from their pedestals, the "old charley" of the beat being either asleep, or feed or frightened into silence. And we must record another of their performances.

Our readers must recollect Mr. William Wallace Currie. He was not himself a man of jokes, and he was about the last man in the world to joke with. Well, he had an office for his business, upon the door of which was inscribed, in the usual way, " WILLIAM WALLACE CURRIE." One morning, upon his arrival, he was utterly horrified to find into what the men of taste had transmuted or translated him. The introduction of a comma and the addition of a single letter astonished him with this new reading of his name and profession, "WILLIAM WALLACE, CURRIER." He joined in the laugh, and there was an end of it. Nor is this the only play upon Mr. Currie's name which we have to record. The late Egerton Smith, to whom be all honour and respect as the father of the Liberal press in this district, and for the honesty and independence and goodness of character which distinguished his long career, once made an admirable hit upon it, which, although it has been in print before, will bear repeating, and is worth preserving. When Mr. John Bourne, as worthy a man as ever lived, was Mayor under the old Corporation, Mr. Currie was one of his bailiffs; and Egerton, being asked on some occasion for a toast or sentiment, following the Lancashire pronunciation of their names, electrified the company by proposing, "*Burn* the Mayor, and *Curry* the bailiff."

And now for one more witticism from Daltera, of whom we have already related so much. It was at the expense of the same Mr. Fogg, whose impalement by Richmond, in an electioneering song, we have immortalised in a former chapter. At a dinner given at Ormskirk by the mess of a regiment of volunteers, or local militia, in which Fogg was a subaltern, Daltera was among the guests. When the cloth was removed, Poor Joe, as was "his custom of an afternoon," became very lively and exhilarated, and, fancying that the other was somewhat dull, suddenly turned to him, and slapping him on the back, exclaimed, "Come, *Fogg, clear up!*" amidst roars of laughter from the party. A veteran officer of the Guards, who happened to be one of the company, still tells this story with the greatest glee and pleasure, and looks back upon the day in question as one of the merriest and most amusing he ever spent.

But we mentioned the name of Mr. William Wallace Currie just now. We must return to him. He was not a man to be casually mentioned and then passed by. He was the eldest son of the great Dr. Currie. His abilities were above mediocrity, and his mind well-cultivated and stored with literature. He may be described as a reading man, in an almost non-reading community. As a speaker, he was ready, but not eloquent. He had more affluence of argument than command of oratory, but he never failed to express himself to the satisfaction of his hearers. In his own circle of society he was much esteemed. As a party leader, he was greatly respected by the public, who regarded him as that *rara avis*, an honest politician. His life confirms the verdict, for, with undoubted influence at his command, he never used it to subserve his own ambition or push his own private interest. That he was never in Parliament may be ascribed to his own modesty. We have heard of more than one borough where the electors would gladly have chosen him to be their representative. Mr. Currie is still remembered with strong affection by his friends, and, when they likewise have passed away, his name will yet survive for many a generation in the title-page of one of the most delightful books which we ever remember to have read. We speak of the *Life of Dr. Currie*, by his son. In reading it, we were charmed and fascinated by the letters and sentiments of the father, and so pleased with the setting in which these jewels were exhibited to us, that our only regret was, that the biographer did not, in executing his task so well, give us more of his own work, but left us to rise from the intellectual treat which he had set before us with an appetite rather whetted than satisfied by the feast which we had been enjoying.

We have said that the reading men in old Liverpool were few. Let us chronicle another of their names, Mr. Alexander Freeland, who still survives amongst us. His inquisitive mind has long since, we may say, made the tour of literature, and the stores of it which he has accumulated are surprising, as he unlocks the treasuries of his mind in the chosen circle before whom "he comes out." We must also place another veteran, Mr. Henry Lawrence, in the ranks of both well-read and literary men. He always had a good seat in the intellectual tournament, and carried a good lance in the tilting of wit. He was never wanting to contribute his part, when present, at "the feast of reason and the flow of soul." To catalogue all his clever sayings would be an endless work. His conversational powers were brilliant and infinite. His wit was keen and of the purest order. We defy the young stagers of to-day to produce his match out of their ranks.

CHAPTER XVI.

T would be a strange picture of "Liverpool a few years since" which did not exhibit Mr. (afterwards Sir) John Gladstone in the foreground of the canvas. He had, in those early days, already taken his position, and was evidently destined to play a conspicuous part in this busy world. We never remember to have met with a man who possessed so inexhaustible a fund of that most useful of all useful qualities, good common sense. It was never at fault, never baffled. His shrewdness as a man of business was proverbial. His sagacity in all matters connected with commerce was only not prophetic. He seemed to take the whole map of the world into his mind at one glance, and almost by intuition to discover, not only which were the best markets for to-day, but where there would be the best opening to-morrow. What was speculation with others was calculation with him. The letters which from time to time, through a long series of years, he sent forth, like so many signal-rockets, to the trading world, under the signature of *Mercator*, were looked upon as oracular by a large portion of the public. And there is little doubt that his authority was often sought and

acted upon, in commercial legislation, by the different Administrations by which the country has been governed during the last half-century. We recollect, many years ago, standing under the gallery of the House of Commons with the late Mr. Huskisson. A sugar question was under discussion, and Mr. Goulburn was hammering and stammering through a string of figures and details, which it was clear he did not comprehend himself, and which he was in vain labouring to make the House comprehend. Mr. Huskisson smiled, as he quietly observed, " Goulburn has got his facts, and figures, and statistics from Mr. Gladstone, and they are all as correct and right as possible, but he does not understand them, and will make a regular hash of it!" Mr. Gladstone was himself in Parliament for some years, and was always listened to most respectfully on mercantile affairs. If he did not make any very distinguished figure, it was because he did not enter upon public life until he had reached an age at which men's habits are formed, and at which they rather covet a seat in the House of Commons as a feather or crowning honour of their fortunes, than as an admission into an arena in which they intend to become gladiators in the strife, and to plunge into all the toils, and intrigues, and bustle of statesmanship. Had our clever townsman entered Parliament at an earlier period, and devoted himself to it, we have no doubt that he would have been found a match for the best of them, and might have risen to the highest departments of the Government. His name is well represented amongst us still. He left four sons behind him, one of whom, the Right Honourable William Ewart Gladstone, is second to no statesman of the day, either in promise or performance, eloquence or abilities. Mr. Gladstone lived in Rodney-street, in a house subsequently taken by Mr. Cardwell, the father of our late clever and gifted representative. So that, by a remarkable coincidence, Mr. W. E. Gladstone and Mr. Cardwell, severally the best men of their standing, first at the university, and now in the list of statesmen, are not only from the same county of Lancaster, which produces so large a proportion of the able men in every profession, but from the same town, and the same street in the same town, and the same house in the same street. Did ever house so carry double, and with two such illustrious riders, before? Nor must we forget to mention Mr. Robert Gladstone, an amiable, kind-hearted man, and one of the most agreeable persons ever to be met with in society, always anxious to please and be pleased.

And there was Dr. Crompton, a fearless, outspoken man, English all over in his bearing. He was the father of the new judge, whose appointment enabled proud Liverpool to say that, as before in Judge Parke, she had furnished the cleverest occupant of the bench, so now she may boast that the two best are both her sons. And what a glorious old fellow, kind, clever, benevolent, well-read, well-informed, and well-disposed was Ottiwell Wood. Who can forget him? His Christian name was a curious and rare one. He was once a witness on some trial, when the judge, rather puzzled in making out his name, called upon him to spell it. Out came the answer in sonorous thunder: "O double T, I double U, E double L, double U, double O, D." His lordship, if puzzled before, was now, if we may perpetrate such an atrocious pun, fairly "*doubled up*," amidst the laughter of the court. We lately, in our travels, met with a gentleman at a party in a distant county. His name, as he entered the room, was announced, "The Rev. Ottiwell ———." When we had been introduced to him, we ventured to ask him where he got it. "Oh!" he replied, "I was so called after an old Lancashire relation of mine, as worthy a man as ever lived, Mr. Ottiwell Wood, of Liverpool." We struck up an alliance, offensive and defensive, and " swore eternal friendship " on the spot. We recollect another gentleman, also called Wood, who once, playing upon the names of some of our fashionables, at a party where he was amongst the guests, thus exclaimed, as he entered the room, " There are, I see, *Hills*, *Lakes*, and *Littledales*, it only wanted *Wood* to perfect the scene."

The Littledales here mentioned were then, as the representatives of the family still are, among the most thriving and prosperous of our leading people. They brought both intelligence and industry to their work. They owed nothing to chance, for they left nothing to chance. And we may truly say of them, that, to whatever branch of commerce or the professions they devoted themselves, they deserved and adorned the success which they achieved. And here we cannot pass on without relating an excellent *bon mot* from the lips of Judge Littledale, the brother of Anthony,

Isaac and George, of the last generation, all, in their different ways, distinguished men amongst our old stagers. Some years since, a gentleman, now one of the most prominent of the rising barristers on the Northern Circuit, had, when almost a boy, to appear before the judge in some legal matter. We do not understand the jargon and technicalities of the law. The opposing party, however, moved that, in a certain case, "the rule be enlarged." To this our young friend demurred, alleging, according to the letter of his instructions, that "he had never, in the whole course of his experience, heard of a rule being enlarged under such circumstances." "Then," replied the judge, with the blandest of smiles, "young gentleman, we will enlarge the rule and your experience at the same time." Never was anything better than this uttered in a court of justice. We heard the story from the young gentleman of such great experience himself. It made an impression on him that will never be effaced; and, doubtless, when a judge himself, he will repeat the anecdote for the benefit of the horse-hair wigs of the next generation.

But, to keep to Liverpool, there must be many yet alive who remember Mr. D'Aguilar among the celebrities and fashionables of the town. A tall, fine-looking, portly man he was. Mrs. D'Aguilar was a charming person in society, the life of every party, and retained to the end of a long life all the vivacity and cheerfulness, as well as the appearance, of youth. She seemed never to grow older. One of their sons, Mr. Joseph D'Aguilar, was decidedly among the wits of the day, and had many a sharp saying and good story attributed to him. Another was General D'Aguilar, who distinguished himself in the Peninsular war, and is the soldier, scholar and gentleman, all three combined in one. Mrs. Laurence, so long the queen of fashion in this locality, was one of their daughters, and, like her brothers, inherited a large portion of intellect from her parents. The patroness of literature in others, she has herself just gone far enough into its realms to excite our regret that she has not gone further. A kindred spirit of Mrs. Hemans, we often wish that she had not only extended her sympathies to that gifted genius, but had, with her own pen, roamed with her, "fancy free," into the regions of poesy, and emulated her inspirations.

And here let us turn aside to embalm the memory of another old stager, well known and much liked in his day, William Rigby. A gentleman in his bearing, endowed with no slight powers of conversation; clever, witty, social, convivial, he was a most popular man in his circle. And, besides, he played a hand at whist second to none, which always made him a welcome guest at houses where card tables appeared. He was a tall, handsome man, with eyes twinkling with the humour and jocularity which made him such an agreeable companion. And shall we forget Devaynes, that nonpareil of an amateur in the conjuring line? Talk not to us of your wizards of the north, or of the south, or of the east, or of the west. Devaynes was worth them all put together. How we have stared in our boyish days, half in wonder and half in alarm, at his wonderful tricks, perfectly convinced in our own mind that such an accomplished master of arts must assuredly be in league with some unmentionable friend in the unseen world. As you sat at table with him, your piece of bread would suddenly begin to walk towards him. Before you had recovered from this astonishment your wine glass would start after it, next your knife and fork, and then your plate would move, like a hen after its chickens, in the same direction. And then how he would swallow dishes, joints of meat, decanters, and everything that came in his way. He was a perfect terror to the market-women, who really believed that he was on the most intimate terms with the unmentionable old gentleman aforesaid. Having made his purchases and got his change for his guinea or half guinea, he would put the coin into their hand, and say to them, "Now, hold it fast, and be sure you have it;" and then, before leaving them, he would add, "Look again, and be certain," when, the hand being opened, there was either nothing in it, or perhaps a farthing, or a sixpence. And even when the joke was over, and he had left the market, they eyed the fairy money both with suspicion and alarm, lest it should disappear, and were never easy until they had paid it away in change to some other customer. How well we remember these things! The performer of them was a quiet, unassuming man, much respected by all who knew him, and certainly one of whom it could not be said that he was "no conjuror."

CHAPTER XVII.

WE have spoken in a former chapter of the oil lamps, which, "few and far between," just made darkness visible, and of the old watchmen, who were supposed or not supposed to be the guardians of our lives and property. The latter deserve another word. The old watchmen, or "Charleys," as they were generally called, were perfect "curiosities of humanity," and the principle on which they were selected and the rules by which they were guided were as curious as themselves. They seem to be chosen as schoolmasters are still chosen in remote villages in the rural districts, namely, because they were fit for nothing else, and must be kept off the parish as long as possible. They were for the most part, wheezy, asthmatic old men, generally with a very bad cough, and groaning under the weight of an immense great coat, with immense capes, which almost crushed them to the ground, the very ditto, indeed of him of whom it was written,

"Pity the sorrows of a poor old man,
Whose trembling limbs have borne him to your door."

They carried a thick staff, not so much a weapon of offence as to support their tottering steps. They had also rattles in their hands, typical, we presume, of the coming rattles in the throat, for they were of no earthly use whatever. Each of them was furnished with a snug box, in which they slept as long as possible. But, if ever they did wake up, their proceedings were of a most remarkable kind. They set forth round their beat with a lantern in their hands, as a kind of a beacon to warn thieves and rogues that it was time to hide, until these guardians of the night had performed the farce of vigilance and gone back to snore. Moreover, like an army marching to surprise an enemy with all the regimental bands performing a grand chorus, they also gave notice of their approach to the same kind of gentry by yelling the hour of the night and the state of the weather with a tremulous and querulous voice, something between a grunt and a squeak, which even yet reminds us of the lines in Dunciad;

"Silence, ye wolves! while Ralph to Cynthia howls,
And makes night hideous: answer him, ye owls."

But, to be sure, the wisdom of our forefathers had a double object in view when they ordered this musical performance to be got up. It not only saved the poor old watchmen from conflicts in which they must have suffered grievously, but it served another purpose, and so " killed two birds with one stone " with a vengeance. Only fancy the happiness of a peaceful citizen, fast asleep after the toils and fatigues of the day, to have his first slumber disturbed that he might be told that it was " half-past eleven o'clock, and a cloudy night," and then, by the time that he had digested this interesting intelligence and was composing himself on his pillow again, to be again aroused to learn that it was now "twelve o'clock, and a starlight morning," and so on every half-hour until day-break. The vagaries of the veritable queen Mab, with "tithe pigs' tails" and all the rest of it, were only more poetical, not the least more rest-disturbing, than the shouts of these bawlers of the night. Truly, the watch committee of those days might have taken for their motto, "Macbeth does murder sleep." And many were the funny tricks played upon these poor, helpless old creatures, by the practical jokers who then so abounded amongst us. Sometimes they would, when caught napping, be nailed up in their boxes, while occasionally, by way of variety, their persecutors would lay them gently on the ground with the doors downwards, so that their unhappy inmates would be as helpless as a turtle turned upon its back, and be kept prisoners till morning. In short, "a Charley" was considered fair game for every lover of mischief to practise upon, and their tormentors were never tired of inventing new devices for teazing and annoying them. Latterly, however, as the town grew larger, the veteran battalions, the cripples, wheezers, coughers, and asthmatics, were superseded by a more stalwart race, who looked as if they would stand no nonsense, and could do a little fighting at a pinch.

The last of these men, whom we recollect before the establishment of the new police, had the beat in the neighbourhood of Clayton-square. Many of our readers must recollect him. He was a six-foot muscular Irishman. "Well, Pat," some of the young ones, who are middle aged gentlemen now, used to say to him, "Well, Pat, what of O'Connell?" On such occasions Pat invariably drew himself up, like a soldier on parade, to his full height, looked devoutly upwards, and then solemnly exclaimed, "There's One above, sir—and—next to him—is Daniel O'Connell!" And it was a name to conjure with in his day! We respected, as often as we heard of it, that poor fellow's reverence for his mighty countryman, and felt that, had we been Irish, we also should have placed that name first and foremost in our calendar of saints, martyrs, patriots and heroes. Who is there now of his name and nation who can rise and say, "Mr. Speaker, I address you as the representative of Ireland." But, forward. How the old times, and the old things, and the old oil-lamps, and the old watchmen have all passed away and disappeared! And the old pig-tails, too, have vanished with them. When we first escaped from petticoats into jacket and trousers, every man, young and old, wore a hairy appendage at the back of his head, called a pig-tail, as if anxious to support Lord Monboddo's theory, that man had originally been a tailed animal of the monkey tribe; for surely our *wholesale re-tailing*, if we may so speak, could have been for no other purpose. Pig-tails were of various sorts and sizes. The sailors wore an immense club of hair reaching half-way down their backs, like that worn by one of Ingoldsby's heroes, and thus described by him,—

"And his pigtail is long, and bushy, and thick,
Like a pump handle stuck on the end of a stick."

Those of the soldiers were somewhat less in magnitude, but still enormous in their proportions. And quiet citizens wore jauntily one little dainty lock, tied up neatly with black ribbon, and just showing itself over the coat collar. It was a strange practice, but custom renders us familiar with everything. At last, however, Fashion, in one of her capricious moods, issued her fiat, and *pigtails* were *curtailed*. But some few old stagers, lovers of things as they were, and the enemies of all innovation, saw revolution in the doom of pigtails, and persevered in wearing them long after they had generally disappeared. The pigtail finally seen in society in Liverpool dangled on the back of ——; but, no, no! never mind his name. He still toddles about on 'Change, and might not like to be joked about it, even at this distance of time. Its fate was curious. Through evil report and good report he had stood by that pigtail as part and parcel of the British Constitution, the very Palladium of Magna Charta, Habeas Corpus, and the Bill of Rights. But the time for a new edition of *The Rape of the Lock* arrived. He dined one day with a party of gay fellows like himself. The bottle went freely round, until, under its influence, our unlucky friend fell fast asleep. The opportunity was seized upon. After some hours' refreshing slumber he awoke, and found himself alone. On the table before him was a neat little parcel, directed to him, made up in silvery paper, and tied with a delicate blue ribbon. What could it be? He eagerly opened it, and found, *Il Diavolo!* that it was his pigtail. "Achilles' wrath," as sung by Homer, was nothing compared with the fury of the wretched man. He stormed, he swore, he threatened, but he could never discover who had been the operator who had so despoiled him, like another Samson, of his pride. Let us hope that remorse has severely visited the guilty criminal. Its work, however, must have been inwardly, for outwardly he is a hale, hearty, cheerful-looking old man, who still carries himself among his brother merchants as if he had never perpetrated such an enormous atrocity.

This, we said, was the last of the pigtails seen in Liverpool society. But we did meet with another, the very *Ultimus Romanorum*, after a lapse of many years, under very peculiar and interesting circumstances. We were walking in Lime-street, when all at once we caught sight of a tall, patriarchal, respectably-dressed man, some three-quarters of a century old, with a pigtail. It was like the ghost of the past, or a mummy from Egypt, rising suddenly before us. The old gentleman, whose pigtail seemed saucily to defy all modern improvements as the works of Satan and his emissaries, was, with spectacles on nose, reading some document on the wall. Being naturally of an inquisitive turn of mind, and especially anxious at that moment to find out what still on earth could interest a pigtail, we stopped to make the discovery. Ha! ha! ha! It nearly killed us with laughter. It was the electioneering address of Sir Howard Douglas. No wonder the old man's sympathies were excited: it was pigtail studying pigtail, Noah holding sweet communion with Methuselah or Tubal Cain. We often marvel within ourselves whether that last survivor of the pigtail dynasty is yet alive, and whether he believes in steam-ships, and railways, and electric telegraphs; whether indeed he believes in the nineteenth century at all, or in anything except Sir Howard Douglas and pigtails.

Hair-powder, which also used generally to be worn in those days, went out of fashion with pigtails. It was in allusion to this practice that the old song laughingly asked,

> " And what are bachelors made of?
> Powder and puff,
> And such like stuff,
> Such are bachelors made of—
> Made of!
> Such are bachelors made of."

Even ladies wore hair-powder. The last, within our memory, so adorned, was Mrs. Bridge, the mother of Mr. James Oakes Bridge, who lived in St. Anne-street, and a fine, stately, venerable lady of the old school she was.

A terrible time was it for hair-dressers, who then carried on a thriving business, when pigtails and hair-powder were abolished at one fell swoop. It was in reality to them like the repeal of the Navigation laws, in idea, to the ship-owners, or free-trade to the farmers. We were amusingly reminded of it only a few weeks since. Being on our travels, with rather a wilderness of hair upon our head, we turned into a barber's shop, in a small town through which a railway, lately opened, runs. The barber had a melancholy look, and seemed to be borne down by some secret sorrow, to which he gave utterance from time to time in the most dreadful groans. At length he found a voice, and rather sobbed than said, "Oh sir, these railways will be the ruin of the country!" Did our ears deceive us? Or was the barber really gone mad? We were silent, but, we suppose, looked unutterable things, for he continued, "Yes, sir, before this line was opened, I shaved twenty post-boys a day from the White Hart, and now if I shave one in a week I am in high luck." Unhappy shaver, to be thus shaved by the march of improvement! And inconsistent George Hudson! thou talkest of the vested rights of shipowners and landlords, and yet didst thou ever stay thy ruthless hand and project a line the less that country post-boys might flourish, and country barbers live by shaving their superfluous beards? O! most close shaver thyself, not to make compensation to thy shavers thus thrown out of bread and beards by thy countless innovations!

But it is time that we should finish this chapter, and we will do so with copying an anecdote touching hair powder, which greatly struck us as we lately read it in the *History of Hungary*. Some great measure was under discussion in the diet of that country, when Count Szechenyi appeared in the Chamber of Magnates, on the 28th of October, 1844, in splendid uniform, his breast covered with stars and ribbons of the various orders to which he belonged. " It is now thirty-three years," said he, " and eleven days since I was sent to the camp of Marshal Blucher. I arrived at the dawn of day, and at the entrance of the tent found a soldier occupied in powdering his hair before a looking-glass. I was rather surprised, but, on passing on a little further, I found a page engaged in the same way. At last I reached the tent of the old general himself, and found him, like the others, powdering and dressing his hair also. 'General,' said I, 'I should have thought this was the time to put powder in the cannon and not in the hair.' 'We hope,' was the reply, 'to celebrate a grand *fête* to-day, and we must, therefore, appear in our best costume.' On that day the battle of Leipsic was fought. For a similar reason, gentlemen, I appear here to-day, dressed in this singular manner. I believe that we are to-day about to perform one of the brightest acts in the history of our nation." The address was received with loud acclamations. But hairpowder and gunpowder have, we believe, long since been divorced, even in the camp. It was inconvenient. It was found, as touching the former, that, on a hot day, it was impossible "to keep your powder dry."

CHAPTER XVIII.

WHETHER we consider the magnificence of its estate, the amount of its revenue, or the extent of its influence, the Liverpool Corporation might ever be compared to a German principality put into commission. We have, in a former chapter, alluded briefly to its state and condition in those old days, when

"All went merry as a marriage bell,"

and no Municipal Reform Bill ever loomed in the distance. But we feel that we must say something more about such an important body. The old Liverpool self-elected Corporation was always looked up to and spoken of with respect from one end of the country to the other. It was, indeed, considered to be a kind of model Corporation by all others, and quoted, and emulated, and imitated on all occasions and in all directions.

We have said that it was self-elected. We must add that it was most exclusive in its character and formation. "We don't shave gentlemen in your line," says the hair-dresser in *Nicholas Nickleby* to the coal-heaver. "Why?" retorted the other, "I see you a-shaving of a baker, when I was a-looking through the winder last week." "It's necessary to draw the line somewheres, my fine feller," replied the principal. "We draw the line there. We can't go beyond bakers." And so it was with the old Corporation. They drew a line in the admission of select recruits into their body, and strictly kept to it. All tradesmen and shopkeepers, and everything retail, were carefully excluded, and classified in the non-presentable "coal-heavers' schedule." But they were not only exclusive in the fashion which has been indicated, but in other ways also. Their line of distinction was more than a separation of class from class. They were not only a self-elected body, but a family party, and carefully guarded the introduction of too many "outsiders," if we may so speak, of their own rank and order in society. They would, indeed, occasionally admit a stranger, without any ties of relationship to recommend him. But this was only done at long intervals, and just to save appearances. Thus, such men as Mr. Leyland, Mr. Lake, and Mr. Thomas Case were, from time to time, introduced into the old Corporation. But extreme care was taken that the new blood should never be admitted in too large a current. For the same reason, that of saving appearances, our ancient municipals, although ultra-Tory in their politics, occasionally opened the door of the Council Chamber to a very select Whig. Nothing, however, was gained for the public by this *quasi*-liberality of conduct. The Whigs, so introduced, generally fell into the ways of the company into which they had been admitted; and it was remarked, that in every distribution of patronage they were at least as hearty and zealous jobbers as the most inveterate Tories. This may have been said enviously. But, at all events, it was said. We are, recollect, writing history, not censure. Human nature is of one colour under every shade of politics. "Cæsar and Pompey very much 'like, Massa; 'specially Pompey."

We have said that, with the exception of the occasional Whig admitted for the sake of appearances, or to be ornamental, the politics of the old Corporators tended to extreme Toryism. They were, nevertheless, divided into two parties, as cordially hating each other as the rival factions in Jerusalem. As their opinions on all great public matters exactly coincided, the apple of discord between them must have been the immense patronage at their disposal, and which was too often considered as the heir-loom of the Corporate families. On one side were the Hollingsheads, Drinkwaters, Harpers, etc. On the other, and at that time, and for years after, the stronger interest, were arrayed the Cases, Aspinalls, Clarkes, Branckers, etc. The latter party owed much of their preponderance to the influence of the great John Foster of that day, who, although not a member of the Council himself, possessed a strange power over its decisions and judgments, and brought to his friends the aid of as much common sense and as strong an intellect as ever were possessed by any individual. But it is not to be supposed that the members of the former Corporation limited their attention and zeal to the battle for patronage and place. Let us do them justice. Considering the immensity of the trust committed to their charge, the fact that there was no direct responsibility to check, control, or guide them, and the sleepy sort of animal which public opinion, now so vigilant and wakeful, so open-eared, open-eyed, and loud-tongued, was in those old stagnant times, our conviction has always been that they performed their duty miraculously well. We are neither their accusers nor eulogists. If they were not perfect, they were not altogether faulty. They expended the town's revenues for the town's good. Their foresight extended to the future as well as the present. They perceived the elements of coming greatness which the port of Liverpool possessed, and laid the foundation, often in the face of as loud clamour and criticism as those days were capable of exciting, of their growth and development. Their successors have but walked in the path which they had opened, and carried out the plans which these Council forefathers had devised. In every part of the town may be seen their works and creations, carried on under the superintendence of the Mr. Foster whom we have mentioned, and of his gifted son, too little appreciated amongst us until he he was beyond the reach of all human praise and applause. On the tablet to Sir Christopher Wren, in St. Paul's, London, it is written, *Si monumentum quæris, circumspice*. And, even so, if we are asked to point out the ever-abiding epitaph which, from generation to generation till the world's last blaze, will uphold the memory of our old defunct Corporation, we should answer "LIVERPOOL." When we are told of their extravagance; when we hear of their nepotism; when their spirit of exclusion is scoffed at; when their ultra politics are ridiculed; let us draw a veil over all and everything, as we contemplate our docks, our churches, our public buildings, and once more exclaim, *Si monumentum quæris, circumspice*. These speaking memorials will remain when all their faults are forgotten!

But we said, just now, that the members of the old Corporation would, from time to time, for the sake of appearances, admit a select Whig or Liberal into their number. This reminds us of a good story, which was circulated at the time, when it was debated among them whether they should or should not elect the present Mr. William Earle. "He is a very clever fellow," said one of them to a grim old banker, thinking thereby to conciliate his favour and win his support. The eulogy had just a contrary effect. "So much the worse," replied old money-bags, "we have too many clever fellows amongst us already." As nobody cried out, "Name, name!" the list of this multitude, this constellation of clever ones, is lost to posterity. And, having mentioned this joke against one of the old Council, let us add another. One day Prince William of Gloucester and his staff of officers were dining with a certain member thereof, who treated them with the best which his house contained and which money could command. When the cloth was drawn, his wines, which were excellent, were not only enjoyed, but highly praised. Being a little bit of a boaster, he perpetrated a small white fib by saying, "Yes! that port is certainly very fine, but I have some better in the cellar." "Let us try it," instantly rejoined a saucy young *aide-de-camp*, amidst the laughter of the company at the alderman being thus caught in his own trap. On another occasion it was said that the presiding genius at a table where His Royal Highness was a guest, thus encouraged his appetite, "Eat away, your Royal Highness, there's plenty more in the kitchen." For the honour of Liverpool refinement, be it known that it was not one of our natives who made this speech, so much more hospitable than polite. It was a gentleman of an aristocratic family, officially connected with the town. But taste was not so fastidious, neither was society so conventional, in those days as they are now. The most expressive word was the word used when it was intended to mean warm sincerity, not empty form.

And what a crowd of the county nobility and the gentry were invited to the Corporation banquets in those old days. There was the venerable Earl of Derby, the grandfather of the present Lord. There was likewise the Earl of Sefton, gay, dashing, and agreeable. Mr. Bootle Wilbraham, and Mr. Bold of Bold Hall, then Mr. Patten, were frequent guests at the Mayor's table. And there was old Mr. Blackburne, who was the county member for so many years in those quiet times of Toryism, when the squirearchy reigned supreme even in the manufacturing districts, An easy-going man, of very moderate abilities, was old Squire Blackburne. He stuck by his party, and his party stuck by him. Many a sugar-plum of patronage fell into the mouths of his family and friends. The Mr. Blundell of Ince, of that day, came frequently amongst us, although, generally speaking, a man of reserved habits, and more given to cultivate his literary tastes than to mix in company. He presented one of the Mayors of Liverpool, Mr. John Bridge Aspinall, with a portrait of himself, half-length, and an admirable likeness. It hung for many years in the drawing-room of the gentleman in Duke-street. Side by side with it was a splendid painting of Prince William of Gloucester, also a gift from His Royal Highness to Mr. Aspinall. Where they are now we know not. But, when dotting down the names of some of the neighbouring gentry who used to look in upon us some forty odd years ago, we must not forget to recall honest John Watkins, "the Squire" of Ditton. Squire Watkins, as many of our old stagers will recollect, was a Tory, if ever there was one in the world. But a noble-souled, true-hearted, generous, hospitable man was he withal, as ever lived, a kind of Sir Roger de Coverley, from the crown of his head to the sole of his foot. And what a house he kept! And how he came out in his especial glory on his coursing days, when all the Nimrods and Ramrods in the county assembled under his roof, and did not resemble a temperance society in the slightest degree. Poor old Squire Watkins! Some terrible Philistine once planted a hedge, or built a wall, we forget which, which trespassed, or was supposed to trespass, an inch or two upon his land. It was just the sort of trifle for two people in the country with nothing to do to quarrel about. The feud, or "fun, grew fast and furious." The squire insisted upon the removal of the encroachment. His opponent refused. Threats followed, defiance succeeded, until, one morning, like Napoleon making his swoop upon Brussels, John Watkins, Esq., took the field at the head of his household troops, the butler, coachman, groom, gardener, etc. At last they arrived on the field of Waterloo. But the opposing Wellington was already there, in position with his followers, himself in front with a double-barrelled gun in his hand. Nothing daunted, the squire, pointing to the encroaching fence which was to be destroyed, cheered on his men to the attack, and the "Old Guard" advanced merrily to the charge. But they were presently brought to a check. "Up Guards!" shouted the hostile Wellington as they approached, while "click" went the cock of his double-barrelled gun, as he raised it to his shoulder, vehemently swearing at the same time that he would shoot the first man who dared to lay hands upon the debatable boundary. The assailants wavered. The squire shouted to them in vain. Even he himself did not like the look of the double-barrelled gun, but, fixing upon John, his butler, to be his Marshal Ney, he encouraged him to the attack. John, however, feeling that "discretion was the better part of valour," hesitated, when his master again cheered him to the fight with this promise of posthumous consolation, "Never mind him, John; if the scoundrel does shoot you, we'll have him hanged for it afterwards." "But please, master," said John, as wisely and innocently, "I'd rather you hanged him first." This was too much. There was no help for it. Hugoumont was saved. Napoleon and his forces retreated, baffled and discomfited, from the field. The squire, peace to his memory, fine old fellow, used often to tell this story in after years, never failing to revile poor John for his cowardice, which lost the day. But we always defended John, and turned the laugh against the squire, by gently insinuating that there was somebody more interested in the quarrel, who was even more prudent than prudent John.

CHAPTER XIX.

THE Church, in the days we are speaking of, was in a very torpid and sleepy state, not only in Liverpool, but throughout the land. None of the evangelical clergy had then appeared in this district, to stimulate the pace of the old-fashioned jog-trot High Churchmen. Neither had Laudism revived, under its new name of Puseyism. Nothing was heard from our pulpits but what might have passed muster at Athens, or been preached without offence in the great Mosque of Constantinople. In fact, "Extract of Blair" was the dose administered, Sunday after Sunday, by drowsy teachers to drowsy congregations. If it did no harm, it did no good. We do not here speak of James Blair, Commissary of Virginia, President of William and Mary College, &c., whose works, little known, contain a mine of theological wealth. We allude to Dr. Hugh Blair, whose sermons, so celebrated in his day and long after, are really, when analysed, nothing better than a string of cold moral precepts, mixed up with a few gaudy flowers culled from the garden of rhetoric. We have often wondered at the praise beyond measure which Dr. Johnson again and again bestowed upon Blair's diluted slip-slop and namby-pamby trifles. He not only spoke of them in the highest terms on every occasion, but thus, in his strange way, once exclaimed, "I love Blair's sermons. Though the dog is a Scotchman, and a Presbyterian, and everything he should not be, I was the first to praise them. Such was my candour." At all events, as we have already stated, "Extract of Blair" was the pulpit panacea universally prescribed at the beginning of the nineteenth century. And we are bound to add, as far as our youthful recollections go, that the majority of the Liverpool clergy in those days were rather below than above the average of mediocrity.

There were some among them, however, whose names are worth recalling. One of the best preachers in those old times was the incumbent of St. Stephen's, Byrom-street, the Rev. G. H. Piercy, a fine fellow in every way. He is still alive at his living of Chaddesley, in Worcestershire, to which he was presented through the influence of old Queen Charlotte. His mother-in-law, the wife of the Rev. Mr. Sharp, then vicar of Childwall, had been about the court in some capacity or other, and it was the good fashion of her Majesty never to forget her friends. Mr. Piercy must have reached the age of the patriarchs at least. Then there was the Rev. Mr. Milner, of St. Catharine's Church, Temple-street, which was removed in making some improvements in that part of the town. Poor Mr. Milner! When not washing his hands, he employed each hour of the day in running after the hour before, and was always losing ground in the race. A kind-hearted man he was, and a pleasant one when you could catch him. He was known as "the late Mr. Milner." The Rev. Mr. Vause preached in those days at Christ Church. He was considered to be a brilliant star in the pulpit, and was indeed a first-rate scholar, a fellow-student with the illustrious Canning, who made many and strong efforts to reclaim him from a course of life which unhappily contradicted and marred all his Sunday teachings. But, even with regard to his sermons, effective and telling as they were made by style, voice and manner, it was found, after his death, when they passed into other hands, that they were chiefly Blair, with others copied from the popular writers of the day. A clergyman, who was to preach before the Archbishop of York, had the choice of them for the occasion. He picked out the one which seemed to him to be the most spicy and telling, and, confident at the time that it was the production of Vause himself, delivered it with mighty emphasis and stunning effect. When it was over, the Archbishop blandly smiled, praised it exceedingly, and then, to the horror and astonishment of the preacher, whispered, " I always liked ———'s sermons," naming the author from whom it was taken. Never did poor jackdaw feel so much pain at being divested of his borrowed plumage.

One of the ablest men, although a mumbling kind of preacher, in those times, was the Rev. Mr. Kidd, who was for so many years one of the curates of Liverpool, a kind of Church serf, who could never rise to be a Church ruler. He had many kind friends, and at many a table which we could mention a plate and knife and fork were always laid for the poor curate. But he ever appeared to us to be an oppressed and depressed man, with a weight upon his spirits which nothing could shake off. There was indeed a romance attached to his history, although he was perhaps the most unromantic looking person that the human eye ever rested upon. He was a brilliant scholar, when a student at Brasenose College, Oxford, and his hopes and ambition naturally aspired to a fellowship. It was supposed to be within his grasp. But how wide is the distance between the cup and the lip! The principal was unpopular, and some of his doings were severely flogged in a satirical poem which appeared without a name. Its cleverness led him to suspect Mr. Kidd, and, without looking for any other proof of the authorship, he became his sworn enemy, and used all his influence, and only too successfully, to turn the election against him. Some love affair, we have also heard, but this was, it may be, only "one of the tales of our grand-father," went wrong with him about the same time. So that, altogether, he was thrown upon the world a sad and downcast man, with blighted hopes and blasted expectations from his very youth, and settled down into the curacy of Liverpool, where he saw more than one generation of inferior men, inferior in scholarship, in learning, in wit, in all and everything, promoted over his head. A pleasant, agreeable, quaint and original companion was poor Kidd amongst his intimates, but tongue-tied in a large party. He saw through the hollowness of the world, and despised it. There was nobody like him for unmasking a sham, and reducing a pretender to his real and proper dimensions. And then his chuckling laugh when he had accomplished such a feat, and impaled the human cockchafer upon the point of his sarcasm! And how bitterly he would allude to his curate's poverty, as, smacking his lips over a glass of old port at some friend's table, and he did not dislike his glass of port, he would tell us that his own domestic allowance of the same was " to smell at the cork on a week-day, and to take a single glass to support him through his duties on a Sunday." Poor fellow! Once upon a time, and such godsends did not often fall to his portion, he had married a couple among the higher orders, and received for it a bank-note which perfectly dazzled him. Then came the marriage breakfast, then the marriage dinner. He was a guest at both, and perhaps took his share of the good things which were stirring. His way home was through the Haymarket. Another gentleman, whose path was in the same direction, hearing a great noise, came up and found our friend fighting furiously for his fee with a lamp-post, and exclaiming, as he struck it with his stick, " You want to rob me of it, you scoundrel, do you? But come on, we'll see!" He was a relation of the celebrated Dr. Kidd, who wrote one of the Bridgewater treatises, and who lately died at Oxford full of years and honours.

Another well-known clergyman in those days was the Rev. Mr. Moss, who was afterwards vicar of Walton for so many years. His share of " the drum ecclesiastic" was decidedly the drum *stick*. But, although a very moderate performer in the pulpit, he had a very good standing in society, and was very much liked in his own "set." Not over witty himself, never was man the cause of so much wit in others, and often at his own expense. He was known in his own circle as "Old England," because "he expected every man to do his duty;" that is, he never met a brother clergyman by any chance without seizing upon him, and asking him if he could do his duty on the next Sunday. In allusion to his convivial qualities and bad preaching, somebody once said of him that "he was better in the bottle than in the wood." This gave him such dreadful offence that he positively consulted his lawyer on the subject of prosecuting the impious blasphemer for a libel. The answer to his enquiry was a hearty laugh on the part of the solicitor himself, with an intimation that he would be laughed out of court also, amidst a shower of jokes about the poet's description of the Oxonians of that day,

"Steeped in old prejudice and older port,"

and be poked with all sorts of fun about *canting*, *recanting*, and *decanting*. The decanter triumphed, although it was a strong allusion to the original offending joke, and the idea of a prosecution was abandoned.

Mr. Moss had an intense horror of all sorts of innovations, and, in the case of the first railway, that between Manchester and Liverpool, this feeling was greatly increased by the fact of his being a large shareholder in a certain canal which might be affected by its success. He was in a fever of excitement and almost raved whenever the subject was mentioned in company. He long clung to the notion that the accomplishment of the line was impossible and fabulous. He magnified every difficulty, dwelt upon every obstacle, and concluded every harangue on the question with the triumphant exclamation, " But, never mind, they cannot do it; Chat Moss will stop it; Chat Moss will stop it." This was said in allusion to that great boggy waste, so called, which for so long a time did really battle with and baffle the skill and efforts of the engineers. On one occasion, when our friend had been holding forth in his usual strain, and finished with a look of defiance at all around him, "*Chat Moss will stop it*," Mr. Thomas Crowther, who was one of the party, quietly answered, "Depend upon it, your *chat*, Moss, will not stop it." This to us is the purest essence of wit, the very *ne plus ultra*ism of it.

"The force of humour can no further go."

Like Pitt's description of what a battle should be, "it is sharp, short, and decisive." It is brilliant, pointed, telling.

There is a joke of almost a similar kind in Boswell's *Life of Johnson*. "I told him" (writes the former) "of one of Mr. Burke's playful sallies upon Dean Marley: 'I don't like the Deanery of Ferns, it sounds so like a *barren* title.' 'Dr. *Heath* should have it,' said I. Johnson laughed, and, condescending to trifle in the same mode of conceit, suggested Dr. *Moss*."

But the wit here is overdone and wire-drawn, until it becomes forced, heavy, and exhausted. Crowther's *extempore* retort beats the laboured efforts of Burke, Boswell, and Johnson, all put together, as it bursts forth, sparkling, glittering, dazzling, on the spur of the moment. "Depend upon it, your *chat, Moss*, will not stop it." We treasure a good thing when we hear it, and love to embalm it. Mr. Crowther, the author of this unrivalled witticism, had a twinkle about the eye which seemed to say for him, that he had many "a shot in the locker," of equal calibre and ready for action. We did not know much of him ourselves, but have always been told that his stores of humour and wit were as rich as they were inexhaustible. The specimen, or, as men say in Liverpool, the sample, which we have given amply justifies such an opinion.

We must not forget to mention, in connection with the Rev. G. H. Piercy, that of the sons of Liverpool worthies under his care in 1804, and who thumbed their lexicons with redoubled zeal when promised a holiday to witness the marching and counter-marching of the "brave army" before his Royal Highness Prince William of Gloucester, in Mosslake fields or Bank-hall Sands, (where are these now?) the following, although in the "sere and yellow leaf," are still fit for active service:—W. C. Ritson, E. Molyneux, Thomas Brandreth, F. Haywood, R. W. Preston, and James Boardman. The Rev. James Aspinall, rector of Althorpe, Lincolnshire, was also long a favourite pupil of the reverend patriarch.

CHAPTER XX.

THE two rectors of those old days were the Rev. Samuel Renshaw and the Rev. R. H. Roughsedge. They were both men past the meridian of life, at the earliest period to which our recollection extends. There was a tradition among the old ladies, that Rector Renshaw in his younger days had been a popular and sparkling preacher of "simples culled" from "the flowery empire" of Blair. We only knew him as a venerable-looking old gentleman, with a sharp eye, a particularly benevolent countenance, and a kind word for everybody. Rector Roughsedge also was a mild, amiable, good-hearted man of the old school, with much more of the innocence of the dove than of the wisdom of the serpent in his composition. He was, in fact, the most guileless and unsophisticated person we ever met with. His studies must have been of books. Certainly they had not extended to the human volume. He was utterly ignorant of the world and the world's ways, thereby strongly reminding us of the great navigator, of whom it was said that "he had been round the world, but never in it," As a proof of this we may mention, that once, when the Bishop of Chester, the present Bishop of London, was his guest, he invited Alexandré, the ventriloquist, to meet him at breakfast. There surely never was a worse assortment than this in any cargo of Yankee "notions." Alexandré, who had a fair share of modest assurance, was quite at home, and made great efforts to draw the bishop into conversation. The latter, however, rather recoiled from his advances, and was very monosyllabic in his answers. Nothing daunted, however, the ventriloquist rattled away quite at his ease, and, amongst other things, assured his lordship that "he had had the honour of being introduced to several of the episcopacy; that, in fact, he had received from more than one of them copies of sermons which they had published, and which he had kept and valued amongst his greatest treasures;" and then finished up with the expression of a wish that he would himself favour him with a similar memento. This was too much, and prompt and tart and cutting was the bishop's answer—"Yes; I will write one on purpose; it shall be on MODESTY!" Vulcan never forged such a thunderbolt as that for Jupiter Tonans himself. It completely floored Alexandré, overwhelming the chaplain and scorching the rector's wig in its way.

And having mentioned the name of Bishop Bloomfield, let us give another specimen of his ability to check any improper intrusion upon his dignity and position. He was a very young man when first he came into this diocese, and some of the older clergy rather presumed upon this. There were at that time many among them who would cross the country, and take a five-barred gate as if it were that fortieth article of which Theodore Hook spoke to the Vice-Chancellor of Oxford. The bishop one day met a number of these black-coated Nimrods. The scene was not far from Manchester. After dinner, some of the old incorrigibles persevered for a long time, with marvellously bad taste, in talking of their dogs and horses, and nothing else. His lordship looked grave, but was silent. At last, one of them, directing his conversation immediately to him, began to tell him a long story about a famous horse which he owned, and "which he had lately ridden sixty miles on the North road without drawing bit." It was the bishop's turn now, and down came his sledge hammer with all the force of a steam-engine. "Ah," he said, with the most cutting indifference, "I recollect hearing of the same feat being once accomplished before, and, by a strange coincidence, on the North road, too: it was *Turpin, the highwayman.*" Warner's long range was nothing to this. It was a regular stunner. The reverend fox-hunter had never met with such a rasper before. He was fairly run to earth, and did not break cover again that night, you may be sure. The idea of a Church dignitary, for such he was, having had Turpin for his college tutor, was a view of the case which he had never studied before, and old *Tally-ho* left the table fully convinced that his spiritual superior was more than his match even at the *lex Tally-ho-nis*. The same annoyance was never attempted again. The lesson had its effect upon more than one.

But to go back to Rector Roughsedge; he also once

perpetrated a joke, and it was so dreadfully heavy that it deserves recording for its exceeding badness. He was a man of strong opinions, prejudices some people would call them. He did not like the evangelical clergy, who so greatly increased in number towards the latter end of his reign in this locality, and, at their expense, he perpetrated the single jest of eighty years. He was at Bangor, on a tour, and, at the same inn there was a large party of the rival section of the Church. They were in the room exactly over the one in which he was sitting, and, as they moved about with rather heavy tread, the old man suddenly exclaimed, " Sure the gentlemen must be walking on their heads!" We do not say much for this ponderous effort ourselves. But it was, we are informed, duly reported at the Clerical Club, and entered among their *memorabilia*. The curates especially relished it as a great joke, a very gem of brilliancy, and would persist in laughing at and repeating it for months and months in all companies, parties and meetings; and their mirth, it was observed, was always particularly jocund and boisterous when the rector himself was present. But who grudges them the enjoyment of their laugh? A poor curate's life is such a career of toil and hardship, that anything which can enliven him, even a rector's jest, should be most welcome. We, at at all events, are not iron-hearted enough to envy their few enjoyments. But it was real happiness to hear the old rector and his old wife talk of their son in India. He was their pride, their boast, their treasure, their idol. We never met with him; but from all that we have heard of him, we believe that there was no exaggeration of praise even in the character which his fond parents drew of him. Everybody endorsed it as fact, not eulogy. But *the* church of churches in that day was St. George's. How we used to rush down to Castle-street, about a quarter of an hour before the service began, to see the mayor and his train march to church! We were never tired of watching that procession. It was super-royal in our estimation. Sunday after Sunday we would gaze at it with never-wearying and still-increasing admiration. Such cloaks they wore! There never were such cloaks. And such cocked-hats! No other cocked-hats ever seemed to be like them. And one man carried a huge sword, which, in our nursery, we verily believed to have been the identical one taken by David from Goliath, although there was a counter tradition, which asserted that Richard the First had won it from a Pagan knight in single combat when in Palestine. We now rather ascribe a "Brummagem" origin to it. And there were other men who carried maces, and various kinds of paraphernalia, which, if not useful, were supposed to be vastly ornamental and magnificent. The mayor himself held what was called a white wand in his hand, which was intended, we opine, to impress the public with the notion that his worship, for the time being, was a bit of a conjurer. But even we little boys knew better than that. Heaven help those dear, darling, innocent old mayors! They knew how to fish up the green fat out of a turtle-mug, and had a tolerably correct idea touching the taste of turbot and lobster-sauce; but as to doing anything in the conjuring line, they were as guiltless on that head as any babe unborn. They would never have run any chance of being burnt for witches. But, nevertheless, it was a very imposing spectacle to see them tramping along Castle-street every Sunday morning to St. George's Church. Our impression always was, that the very Gauls who paid such small respect to the Roman senate would have trembled with awe at such a sight. Such was our enthusiasm that, often as we witnessed it, we still, on our return home, assembled all our brothers and sister, and arraying ourselves in table-cloths and great-coats, with the shovel, tongs and poker carried before us as our official insignia, performed a solemn march upstairs and down stairs, from garret to cellar, until interrupted by some older member of the family, who looked upon our imitations to be as sinful as sacrilege or "flat blasphemy" itself.

And what a congregation there used to be at St. George's in those days! It was a regular cram. Every corporator had a pew there, and felt himself in duty bound to attend out of respect to the mayor. And how gay and smart were the bonnets and dresses of their wives and daughters. There was one seat in particular which always divided our attention with the service. It was constantly full of children, who were not at all more unruly than the rest of us. But their mother, who was of a very Christian and pious turn of mind, seemed to be of a different opinion; for when she thought nobody was watching her (but we were always watching her), what sly opportunities she would take of pulling their hair, treading on their toes, and pinching them in all directions. Pinching was the favourite mode of dealing with them. How we used to speculate during the sermon upon the consequences of her practices! We wondered that they did not cry out. And then we wondered more whether hair-pulling, toe-treading, and pinching were apostolical receipts for training young Christians. And then we thought within ourselves that they would be quite bald in so many years at the rate of so many hairs pulled out every Sunday; and then we used to long to know how many square inches of their skin had turned black and blue under the pinching process, and to speculate whether their fond mother boxed their ears, or set them a chapter to learn, or kept them without their dinner when she got them home, and found that we had grinned them out of all memory of the text as we telegraphed them out of our pew to let them know that we were quietly enjoying the fun in theirs.

And what a muster of carriages there always was at St. George's, to take the corporators and fashionables home after service. How the coachmen squared their elbows, and how the horses pranced, and how the footmen banged-to the doors! And then when "all right" was heard, how they dashed off, to the right and left, some taking one turn and some the other, down narrow old Castle-ditch, and so into narrow old Lord-street, down which they flew "like mad," until the profane vulgar called these exhibitions " the Liverpool

Sunday races!" And what a crowd of dandies and exquisites always assembled on the Athenæum steps, not to discuss the sermon, we fear, but to criticise the equipages as they rattled by, and, when they were gone, to pass judgment upon the walkers, their dress, appearance, etc. The ladies, we recollect, invariably pronounced this phalanx of quizzers to be an accumulation of "sad dogs" and "insufferable puppies;" but it always struck our young mind that it was very odd, if they really thought so, that they did not avoid them by ordering their carriages to be driven, or themselves walking, some other way. If the moth flies into the candle more than once, we must presume that it does not dislike the operation.

CHAPTER XXI.

WE spoke, in the last chapter, of St. George's as the church which the mayor and corporation always attended. Once, when Mr. Jonas Bold was Mayor, it happened that Prince William of Gloucester was present. By a strange coincidence, which somewhat disturbed the seriousness of the congregation, the preacher for the day took for his text, "Behold, a greater than Jonas is here." Both Mayor and Prince, we believe, as well as the discerning public, fancied that there was something more than chance in the selection of so very telling and apposite a text. It reminds us of the Cambridge clergyman, who, when Pitt, Chancellor of the Exchequer, while yet almost a boy, attended the University Church, preached from the words, "There is a lad here which hath five barley loaves and two small fishes; but what are they among so many?"

Some years since the Duke of Wellington, attended by a single *aide-de-camp*, walked into a Church at Cheltenham. Here there could have been no design; he was totally unexpected. But, when the text was announced, out came the startling words, " Now, Naaman, captain of the host of the king of Syria, was a great man with his master and honourable, because by him the Lord had given deliverance unto Syria: he was also a mighty man in valour, but he was a leper." This chance shot evidently told. A grim smile seemed for a moment to gather upon the features of the "Iron Duke," as he cast an intelligent look at his companion, who telegraphed him in return with an equally knowing glance. They were both particularly attentive to the sermon, in which there were many hard hits, which might have been made to order, as they seemed to be as applicable to Duke Arthur as to Duke Naaman.

But it is time that we should speak of the clergymen attached to St. George's Church, in the days we are writing of. They were rather a superior lot. Archdeacon Brooks was one of them, and already looked upon as a very promising young man. The Rev. T. Blundell was another. He used to bring out occasionally, in preaching, very odd things in a very odd manner, and sometimes very original things in a very original manner. The Rev. Jas. Hamer was another of the preachers at St. George's, and very admirable sermons he gave. He was a sedate, grave, serious looking man, a fair scholar, and had a good place in society. He was a fellow of Corpus Christi College, Oxford, and, according to the universal anticipation, would have been its next head, had he lived. But he was cut off in the prime of his days, when all the toils and difficulties of his career were surmounted, and, to human judgment,

> "The world was all before him, where to choose
> His place of rest."

But here we must make room on our canvas for the portrait, if we can draw it, of one of the most remarkable men whom Liverpool has ever produced. We speak of Dr. Frodsham Hodgson, who, in our young days, was also among the St. George's preachers. His manner was pompous, and he had a catch in his voice which may still be traced among Oxford men of the old school, some having adopted it from admiration, and others having mimicked it until they could not get rid of it. Never was the truism, that "a prophet is not a prophet in his own country," more wonderfully illustrated than in the case of Dr. Hodgson. Here, in Liverpool, he was neither known, valued, nor appreciated. He visited chiefly, when amongst us, with the corporation, and those who met him came away with the impression that they had spent their time with a very agreeable and pleasant person, a jovial companion, with great conversational powers, and, for a book-worm, wonderfully at home on every subject started and spoken of on every occasion. This was the opinion generally formed of him, this and nothing more. Our municipal magnificos, while condescendingly patronising and listening to their chaplain, never seemed for a moment to feel that Jupiter himself was among them in disguise.

But let us change the scene to the University of Oxford. Ha! who comes here? "Richard's himself again." "The king's once more at home." It is the principal of Brasenose College, the same Dr. Hodgson whom we lately saw in Liverpool; but, *Quantum mutatus ab illo Hectore*, he is here another and a different man. He is in the scene of his glory, his triumphs, and his celebrity, among those who honour, respect, and look up to him, and who are proud to be the followers of such a leader. He stood out from among them as one of nature's true nobility. Magnificent in his manner and bearing, princely in his tastes, and habits, and notions, and ideas, a scholar in every sense of the word, thoroughly acquainted with, at home in, every branch of literature, and familiar with all the mysteries and workings of the human volume, he was exactly the person to perform a great part wherever his lot of life had been cast. Accordingly he was a potentate even among the self-elated potentates of the University. His will was law. His *sic volo sic jubeo* was supreme. He ruled without a rival near the throne. From time to time murmurs were heard against the autocrat, and the whispering tokens of a coming storm were frequently perceived. But mind triumphed over matter. He always contrived to crush the incipient rebellion, and to rise, like another Antæus, refreshed and strengthened from the struggle. And we may add here that his ambition was as unbounded as his talents were great and brilliant. The force of his genius, the power of his tact, and the extent of his influence were never so remarkably proved as in the management and clever combinations by which, with the help of Tory tools subdued to his will, he contrived to return the Whig Lord Grenville, as Chancellor of the University of Oxford, against Lord Eldon, the most powerful opponent whom it was possible for Toryism to have selected for the struggle in those days of its supremacy. The time at last arrived when Dr. Hodgson was marked for the next elevation to the episcopal bench, and he was spoken of for either an English bishopric or an Irish archbishopric. But who can dive into the secrets of to-morrow? At the moment when to his friends and family it seemed certain that all their fond hopes and anticipations were about to be realised, he was suddenly attacked by the fatal illness which brought him to the grave in a few days. To the end of his life he retained all his influence over the University, and, when he departed, it was as if Gulliver had been taken from Lilliput, and the Lilliputians left to themselves. Nothing soaring above the common place of mediocrity has since shown itself among the college heads and rulers. When we heard of his death, we exclaimed,

> "He was a man, take him for all in all,
> We shall not look upon his like again."

Nor have we since had occasion to recall the exclamation, either with regard to men in the Church or out of the Church. And we have yet a more pleasing sight in which to view the character of Dr. Hodgson, namely, as he was seen in the domestic circle. It was a positive treat to see him, with all the pomp and pride of the outer world thrown off, in the bosom of his family. Never was there so kind and affectionate a husband, never so fond, and tender, and indulgent a father. In his home, surrounded by those whom he loved, and who loved him, he seemed to forget at once all things beyond, and to leave behind all the aspirations and longings, pains and pleasures, sweets and bitters of ambition. You had thought him, perhaps, a cold and calculating competitor in the race of intriguing rivals for promotion. You had watched with pleasure his splendid career at college and in the University. You had admired him as a scholar, been dazzled by his literary attainments, or struck by his tact and bearing as a polished and finished courtier, a character on which he laid such stress that it was a frequent saying with him, that, "in his estimation, manner was everything, next to religion." But it was in the enjoyment of his home, to him not figuratively, but really " home, sweet home," that you were at once startled and delighted by seeing him in the best and most amiable point of view. Here the exquisite nature of the man was beheld in in all its glory, affectionate, gentle, and earnest, with a heart overflowing with every kindly feeling and domestic virtue. " The most loveable man, perhaps," as some one has written of the poet Moore, " that ever lived, judging him in the shade of his own home, apart from the artificial glare of society." All selfishness was there renounced. His happiness was in the happiness of those around, and that those moments, stolen from his active and proud career, were the sweetest and most delicious of his life it was impossible to doubt. He must, like every other public man, often and often have been taught the bitter truth that " all is not gold that glitters." But, whenever the bubble of popular applause in which he so delighted was grasped, only to burst in his hand, whenever the seemingly gorgeous gems of ambition turned out to be mere trash and tinsel, when they had passed from a dream or a hope into realities, he could dwell upon his home treasures, which were to him his greatest "joys for ever," far more precious to him than the world's most approving smiles, and his best and truest consolation if ever it frowned upon him. We respect and honour the name of Dr. Hodgson, when we recollect him as the scholar, the gentleman, and the clergyman; but we love it and fondly dwell upon it when we recall his memory as the husband and the father. How little was he known and how ill understood in his native town! and how few amongst us even remember him or his name at all! And yet Liverpool, and she has been a fruitful parent of worthy children, never had a son of whom she had more cause to be proud than FRODSHAM HODGSON. We have but feebly sketched a character which, we trust, some stronger pen will undertake to delineate in all its fair proportions and colossal dimensions. Until this is done there will be a gap in biography which certainly ought to be supplied, and the sooner the better.

CHAPTER XXII.

AN election was an election, indeed, in those days. It was not merely a rush to the hustings for a few short hours, and then all over. There was no getting the lead by ten o'clock in the morning, and winning at once by making a good start. Votes were then taken by tallies, or tens, each tally marching to the hustings, with a band of music and colours before it, and each party bringing up its tally in its regular turn. The curiosity, and excitement, and suspense, and anxiety were kept up, day after day, until there was a grand smash at last on one side or the other; in other words, until " no tally " forthcoming in its turn betrayed weakness, and proclaimed that it was U P with somebody. An election, then, in those times, was a great and solemn affair with our jolly old freemen, who had the vote-market all to themselves, no intrusive ten-pounders having yet been thrust upon the constituency. How well we recollect the hurly-burly of some of those old elections. There were two sections of the Tory party always in the field, the green, or Tarleton party, and the blue, or Gascoigne and " Townside " party. But, at a pinch, they always coalesced against the pinks or Reformers. Among the greens were the Drinkwaters,

Hollinsheads, Harpers, etc. Foremost in the ranks of the blues were the Fosters, Cases, Aspinalls, Gregsons, Branckers, Clarkes, Leylands, etc. And the pinks also numbered a gallant phalanx to do battle for them in every struggle, Earles, Lawrences, Croppers, Rathbones, Roscoes, Curries, Harveys, Mathers, *cum multis aliis*. And how Jack Backhouse and Corf, the butcher, used to head up the greens on horseback, in Castle-street, both they and their horses bedizened all over with ribbons of their favourite hue! And how popular old Tarleton was with the fishwomen! And then how the Tories would shout for "Negro-slavery, and no Popery!" And the Reformers had "Civil and Religious Liberty!" written on their flags. And how well we remember one, long before the opening of the trade to the East Indies, on which was inscribed, "The China trade for ever." This was quite beyond the geography of the party who carried it; for, supposing it to be an allusion to a competition between home-made crockery and Dresden china, they had, by way of illustration, or commentary, hung the flagstaff round with all sorts of specimens of plates, and dishes, cups and jugs, and so forth. Many a laugh was raised at their expense, as they marched about in blessed ignorance of their blunder.

On one occasion, as if foreshadowing events which were to happen half-a-century later, a big loaf or Free Trade candidate took the field, to the great delight of all the hungry non-electors. It seems but as yesterday when, patriotically braving all the pains and penalties attached to such an audacious proceeding, we escaped from the nursery to clap our little hands, and set up our little shout, as we followed the music and yellow banners of the champion of cheapness and plenty to his house in Kent-square. His name was Chalmer, and he was the father of the venerable, and worthy, and clever doctor and town councillor of that name. Sir Isaac Coffin, too, once made his appearance here just before an election. It was, of course, suspected that he had a design upon the borough. If he had, the intention died in the egg. No chicken ever was hatched out of it. Richmond, however, instantly fired at him with a squib, which opens in this unceremonious fashion :—

> " Sir Isaac Coffin's come to town, not to please the lasses,
> But to gull the Whigs, a set of stupid asses."

A good story is told against Sir Isaac on the other side of the Atlantic. He once made a bet that he would find a given number of gigantic alderman lobsters of the weight of thirty pounds each. It happened not to be in the lobster season, and the monsters were not forthcoming on the appointed day. Sir Isaac, however, not liking to lose his money, sent in certain depositions to the stakeholders from fishermen on the coast, stating that they had frequently met with lobsters of the required weight; to which this pithy answer was returned, " Depositions are not lobsters."

The old freemen of those days were worthy grandsires of their present worthy grandsons. Some of them were witty rogues in their generation. One of them, on the eve of an election, when in a state of intoxication, asked one of the Hope family to give him a five pound note for his vote. The demand was indignantly rejected. "Then," rejoined the incorrigible fellow, "if you will not give it me, lend it me, and you may believe I will return it on any day you fix." Mr. Hope shook his head with resolute incredulity. "Ah," said the offended elector, staggering away, "they may call you HOPE, but hang me if you have either *faith* or *charity* in your composition."

But we must not pass by, without some remarks, the two soldier representatives who so long sat for Liverpool in the House of Commons. General Tarleton was a fearless old guerilla of the American war, in which his achievements, successful or otherwise, proved him to be as brave as the sword he wore, and were more like the creations of romance than the realities they were. He was open, frank, and free, with many qualities to recommend him to popular favour, but no more fit to represent the mighty interests of Liverpool, even in those days, than any child of three years old taken out of the street. He had not one point of the statesman in his whole character. He was as capriciously selected as he was capriciously ejected by his friends. He was originally adopted without a single recommendation. He was finally repudiated without a fault or failure in addition to those which had marked his career from the first. We have heard many things laid to the charge of our old freemen, but they never appeared in so bad a light to us as when, at the bidding of their employers, or under some other influence, they almost to a man turned their backs with freezing indifference upon a candidate towards whom, on all previous occasions, they had affected to feel an enthusiasm amounting to positive frenzy. Human nature was never presented to us in so despicable a point of view. Poor old Tarleton. We never felt a sympathy for him except when he was thus suddenly victimised by popular caprice, his former worshippers flying from their idol. And why? Tell it not in Gath, if you like, but we will tell it in Liverpool; because the rich men of his party had set up another image, and he presented himself for their votes *in formâ pauperis*, Say not, or we shall laugh at you, that he was rejected to make way for the brilliant Canning. Aye, Canning, all honour and glory to his memory, was the most brilliant of all the brilliant stars that ever shone in this lower world of ours. But we never loved brilliancy from our hearts in Liverpool. We have tolerated it at times for the sake of other qualities by which it has been accompanied, but we were always anxious to get rid of it as soon as possible. Liverpool looks upon able and clever men as Athens looked upon Aristides. Mediocrity suits our temper best.

But we spoke of General Tarleton's military colleague, the Castor to his Pollux, General Gascoigne. "The old general," as the latter was familiarly called, was a remarkable instance of how little is required to make a legislator. He had all the unfitness of General Tarleton without his dashing and brilliant exploits as a soldier, to veneer and varnish over the preter-pluperfect common-place of his character. He was an ignorant and illiterate man. This may, perhaps, be ascribed to the early age at which he had joined the army. At all events, his education must have been more in the school of Mrs. Malaprop than of Dr. Syntax. His highest attribute was a species of cunning, which sometimes did for him what greater talent has failed to do for other persons. He was a man of intense selfishness. His gratitude was of that peculiar kind which burns with a white heat glow for benefits to come, but looks with cold and freezing eyes upon favours received. He treated his friends as he did his gloves, that is, he wore out both, and then cast them from him. He constantly forgot his supporters at the last election, to coquet with those who, he hoped, might help him at the next. But such a game could not be played for ever.

General Tarleton was, we said, in his summary expulsion from the representation, the victim of ingratitude. When General Gascoigne's turn came, he was justly punished for his ingratitude towards so many of his best friends. He had most industriously earned the fate which overtook him. His immediate predecessor in the seat for the borough was his brother, Bamber Gascoigne, of Childwall-hall, whose only daughter and heiress married, at a later period, the Marquis of Salisbury. Bamber was a man of a very different stamp and calibre from his brother. He was a good specimen of the gentleman of the old school, and very much superior generally to the country squires of his day. His tastes were refined and literary. He was a thoroughly educated and well-read person. He was at once proud and courteous in his manner, and aristocratic in his bearing. His habits attached him more to his library than to the arena of the House of Commons, and he, consequently, did not kill himself with toiling in the cause of his constituents. On some occasion, a deputation of our merchants waited upon him to remonstrate upon some alleged lack of zeal in their behalf. The interview was not a pleasant one. The member received the remonstrants with either too little humility or too little courtesy. As they grew warmer, he became colder and stiffer. The end of the matter was that they did not exactly part company in a gale of wind, but, while they gave him notice to quit, they relented so far that they told him that, out of respect to a family which had so long represented the town, they would, in depriving him of his seat, transfer it to his younger brother, the redoubtable general. It was a pity, for he had every quality which the other wanted. The thing, however, was done, and for years Bamber Gascoigne was a stranger to the town for which he had once sat in parliament. He had received a blow, an insult he deemed it, which he could never forget, although towards the end of his life he seems to have forgiven it, and once more, to some small extent, had some intercourse with Liverpool society. Mrs. Gascoigne, his wife, however, as excellent and kind-hearted a person as ever lived, always took a most lively and remarkably fussy interest in our elections. She felt that, if her husband could not retain the representation of Liverpool, still it was a prize worth keeping in the family. It may be that her husband thought so too, but he was too proud and impassive to show it.

But let us return to the "Old General." In politics he was a Tory, "thorough and thorough." He never flinched nor wavered, but followed the banner of his party "for better and for worse," through good report and evil report, to the close of his career. He was once, indeed, dreadfully puzzled when a schism occurred amongst the leaders of Toryism. On that occasion he wrote a letter, said to be still in existence, to a leading friend in Liverpool, in which he thus expressed himself:—" Dear ——, I cannot as yet see my way clearly, or make out which section will prevail, and obtain the government. Until that is decided, I shall vote *according to my conscience.*" It is refreshing to discover even these brief traces of a conscience in a hack politician of the old school. We have already observed that the education of the General had not been too carefully cultivated. He once, in the House of Commons, gave a remarkable proof of his deficiency, to the great delight of the young and waggish portion of our legislators. In some debate, touching the extension of political privileges to the dissenters, one of the orators had dwelt eloquently upon the beauty and loveliness of harmony and union between different sects. Gascoigne rose to do a bit of bigotry for his friends, but, being most *singular* in his notions of the *plural* of the word used, thus commenced his reply, " I hate to hear all this cant about the harmony and union which ought to exist between different *sexes*." He got no further. A regular "Hurrah" of laughter burst from every corner of the House. On it went gathering strength as it advanced, explosion after explosion, thunderclap after thunderclap, in the wildest confusion. The younger members shouted with glee and merriment. Grave old statesmen held their sides, and were nearly thrown into fits in the vain endeavour to repress their mirth. Mr. Speaker himself, after an idle attempt to check the row, led the chorus until the very mace danced upon the table, and every hair of his wig stood on end in horror at the profanation. Never was such a scene enacted before or since in the House of Commons; and what gave the greatest zest to the whole thing was, that the General seemed to be unconsciously innocent and ignorant that he was the cause of the unusual commotion which was going on. It was the greatest performance of his life. In parting with him, we may as well add here, that, from a quality which we have before ascribed to him, he was called, his name being Isaac, "Cunning Isaac," both by friends and foes.

In finishing the chapter, we would remark that subscriptions for electioneering expenses were raised in those times after a fashion which, we trust and believe, does not prevail at the present day. The figure written in the list was understood to be the price of the patronage to be received in return. There was a regular scale. This was corruption in its most unblushing and unscrupulous form.

CHAPTER XXIII.

UR shops frequented by the fashionables were "few and far between" in those old times. We had not then reached the bustling age of competition, colossal plate-glass windows, and "selling off under prime cost;" and so, as the Irishman said, making our fortunes by the amount of business transacted. One shop greatly patronised by the ladies was Wilson's, near the old dock, that is, what was the old dock, but which was most unwisely filled up. The Custom-house now stands where the Jack Park, and the Mary, and the Lovely Nancy once rested on the waters after achieving their homeward voyage, and poked their bowsprits into the windows of the opposite houses, which were inconveniently near. Wilson dealt in all sorts of ladies' wares, clothing, linen, table-cloths, &c.

At the bottom of Duke-street there was a kind of ornamental or nick-nack shop, kept by a Miss Gregson, who had a monopoly of that line of business. At the corner of King-street and old Pool-lane, now South Castle-street, there was a famous haberdashery and silk shop, presided over by a most respectable person, Mr. Orton. His private residence was in St. Anne-street, opposite to Mr. Boardman, and next door to Mr. Huddleston, whose son, John, lived there in 1790, and lives there still in 1852. There was another in Castle-street, kept by Mr. Bernard or Brennand, almost as celebrated. We remember this one more particularly, as several of the young men who stood behind the counter subsequently embarked as merchants in different lines of business, and were some of them eminently successful. One of them died not very long ago, and is understood to have left an almost princely fortune behind him.

Danson was then, and for many a long year afterwards, our *Magnus Apollo* in the hair-dressing line. Never was there such a good-natured, polite, kind soul as Danson. He was the most talkative of haircutters, and they are genearally a talkative race. What demand he used to be in on the eve of a ball or a great party in those days, when so much stress was laid upon curls and wiggery! Many a good story was told at his expense; but gentlemen of his profession have ever been so martyred. He was said to be of a very inquisitive turn of mind, and much given to fathoming the why and the wherefore of every novelty and mystery which came in his way. This propensity once led him into an awkward scrape. Shower-baths were not as general and everywhere affairs then as they are now. Our Apollo, once summoned to put some lady patroness into curls, had, upon his arrival, to wait some little time in the ante-room. A tall, oblong, curtained sort of box met his eye. What could it be? He cautiously opened the door, peeped and peeped into it, but could make nothing of it. A string dangled from above. And what was that for? Our philosopher, bent upon experiment, took it into his hand; pulled it; and fiz—souse—splash! he was not exactly caught like a rat in a trap, but down came Niagara upon his devoted head, as quick as lightning, and as loud as thunder. The victim screamed; while, to enjoy the sport, in rushed the lady, and the lady's maid, and the lady's husband, and Prim, the butler, and John, the footman, and Jane, the housemaid, and Molly, the cook, and Sally, the scullion, and the children, and the lap-dog, and there was such laughing and such barking as human misfortune never called forth before. Merry mourners at a funeral never equalled them in their uproarious enjoyment. There had not been a richer scene since Falstaff was "carried off in a buck basket," and then, as he described it, "thrown into the Thames and cooled, glowing hot, in that surge, like a horse-shoe; think of that, hissing hot, think of that, Master Brook." It was enough to give a man hydrophobia for life.

Our old stagers must also recollect the Liverpool Hunt of those days, famous, far and wide, for its good riders, good horses, and good dogs. It was a glorious sight to the lovers of the sport to see them turn out when

> "A southerly wind and a cloudy sky
> Proclaimed it a hunting morn."

Mr. Haywood, who lived in St. Anne-street, was a leading Nimrod among them. It was a treat to have a walk through his stables. And there was Mr. Joseph M'Viccar, with his slight, elegant, and compact figure, who was second to no man in crossing the country. Nor must we forget another of them, Peter Carter. Peter was an original in his way. He loved a good horse and always rode one, and knew how to do it. When George the Fourth, then Prince of Wales, visited Liverpool, Peter had a gray horse, of which he was very fond and very proud. It might have been the very nag of which it was written,

> "But the horse of all horses that rivalled the day
> Was the squire's Neck or Nothing, and that was a gray."

We rather think, if our memory does not play us fast and loose, that Carter was a member of the Liverpool Light Horse, which formed the escort of his royal highness from Knowsley to the town. At all events, the prince saw the horse, and was much struck with it. The price was asked. A hundred guineas was the answer. It was to be a bargain. A few days afterwards a royal groom made his appearance at Peter's stable. He had come for the horse. Now it so happened that there was a general impression that the prince's credit with his banker was not very extensive at that time. Peter was awake to this.

> "Where 's your money?"
> "I 've forgot," etc.

The groom, as we said before, had come, but the hundred guineas were not forthcoming. With some people the wish of royalty is said to be a command, but nothing less than an order upon the bank would satisfy Peter Carter. No other "Open Sesame" would unlock his stable door. We will not assert that our old acquaintance was familiar with the axiom which teaches that "there is no royal road to mathematics;" but he was sagacious enough to feel that there was no royal way in horse dealing. "A bird in the hand is worth two in the bush." He had possession of the horse; he might never get the money. It was, therefore, to use a vulgar phrase, "No go with him;" that is, he would not let the horse go. The groom took his leave, greatly astonished and disgusted, and nothing more was ever heard of the matter. And all that we can say of it is, that Peter was no courtier, but a sensible man of business, while the gray continued to adorn the Liverpool, instead of the Royal, Hunt.

And then there was Abraham Lowe, queer, quaint, odd, original, eccentric, funny, unequalled Abraham Lowe, the huntsman to the pack. How well we recollect him! When we were a boy in buttons, that dress which ladies' pages now usurp and monopolise, we had a taste for haunting and strolling about in the quiet lanes in the neighbourhood of Childwall. We used to fish in some of the pits in that quarter, that is, we threw in our line and hook, and watched them by the hour. But the result was always, like a bad banker's account, "No effects." Probably there were no fish in our favourite ponds. We have often thought so since. But "hark back" to Abraham Lowe! How we did reverence and respect him! And how we would listen to his peculiar stories, told in his own peculiar way! We liked and honoured everything at Childwall. We had a strong regard for that fine old fellow, Mr. Clarke, of Stand-house. We rather looked up to the vicar, Mr. Sharpe. We stood in some sort of awe of Bamber Gascoigne, of the Hall, with his proud and grave bearing. It was our pleasure to watch the members of the Childwall Club, at their afternoon sports, with bow and arrow. It was our delight, when our pockets could afford it, to devour the exquisite pies which they made at the inn near the church. But the vicar and the squire, Mr. Clarke, the club, and even the pies, all paled into nothingness when compared with Abraham Lowe. We used to wonder whether Nelson and Julius Cæsar could be at all like him. His horse always seemed to be the best horse in the world, and his whip the nicest whip, a little greasy or so, but that looked knowing. And with what especial reverence his hounds regarded him! They seemed to know and feel that there was but one Abraham Lowe in the world, and that he was their huntsman, and that they were his hounds. And how he would top the fences and gates! Nothing could stop him! And what a voice he had when he shouted "Tally ho!" or gave the "Hark!" when a hare was up before the dogs. And who so acquainted with every art, and trick, and dodge of his craft! How he always hit upon the right spot for affording the best sport! And who like him for recovering a lost, or keeping the hounds up to a cold, scent? Poor Abraham Lowe! It seems but yesterday that he stood before us with his tall, wiry figure; all sinew and bone, not a superfluous ounce of flesh about him. What a treasure of a character he would have been to Scott, or Dickens, or Thackeray! Reality is more wonderful than fiction. These word-painters never delineated anything equal to Abraham Lowe. Poor Abraham! he was run to earth himself at last, and we fear that, in his declining years, the world did not smile upon him as it did at first. Long after the time of which we have been speaking, we have seen him occasionally creeping about the streets of Liverpool with his limbs stiffer than they were of yore, his old top-boots terribly worn and patched, and his old red coat awfully stained and soiled. We always had a passing word with him, for the sake of "auld lang syne." He never seemed to be downhearted, but maintained his independent character to the end of his days. There are, we trust, other old stagers left who will join us in saying, "Peace to the memory of old Abraham Lowe."*

And talking of hunters, we were, in those days, occasionally visited by Nimrods of another sort, of

---

* We copy with much pleasure the following note, which appeared in the *Albion* of the 2nd August, 1862:—"OLD ABRAHAM LOWE.— *A Subscriber* says, 'The writer of the interesting papers upon *Liverpool a Few Years Since* has fallen into an error, which I wish to correct. "Old Abraham Lowe, the huntsman," did not end his days in poverty, but enjoyed a small annuity, which was purchased for himself and wife for their joint lives, by subscription among those who had enjoyed his services for so many years. This fund was, I believe, under the care of the Messrs. Fletcher, of Allerton, by whose kindness and attention the latter days of the veteran were well protected.'"

the very race of the Centaurs themselves. We speak of the Cheshire squires of the old times, before railways were thought of, and when Macadam was a theorist. A Cheshire squire was then a remarkable peculiarity of the "old-fashioned English gentleman." He was proud of his family, of his house, of his grounds, of his horses, of his dogs, and of everything belonging to him. But he was especially proud of his county, and his county was especially fond of him. He seldom passed beyond its borders, except when a fox led the hounds over them. He was constant in his attendance at the Hoo-green Club, where the conversation, not dazzlingly intellectual, generally ran upon proud Cheshire, and its right to be called proud Cheshire, with an occasional episode upon horses, dogs, the crops, the weather, and "the next meet." A long frost in the winter was a terrible interruption to the comforts and habits of these gentlemen. At such times they would, although not often, get as far as Liverpool, to lay in a stock of wine and so forth. You might always know them. The Cheshire squire, when perambulating our streets in the old times, wore a low crowned hat, a cut-away green coat, and a stripy sort of waistcoat, buckskins, and top boots, looking very like what, in these days, is vulgarly called "a regular swell." There were some curious characters, very original, spicy, and eccentric among them. How well we recollect old Sir Peter Warburton. He was for many years the master of the Cheshire Hunt. For some reason or other there was not much love lost between him and the people of Knutsford. One day, when the hounds were at fault, a sudden "Tally ho!" was heard from a distant hill. "Who's that?" said the baronet. "A Knutsford man," answered the huntsman. At the same moment a favourite dog gave tongue, and led off the pack in another direction. "Hark to Jowler! hark! hark!" shouted Sir Peter, adding with a most uncomplimentary emphasis, "I'd rather believe that dog than any man in Knutsford!"

Sir Harry Mainwaring was another of these antediluvian worthies and wonders. He took the direction of the hounds after the death of Sir Peter. He was a hard rider, and loved his glass of port after the fatigues of the day. At one time his constitution was supposed to be somewhat shaken by these combined labours of love, and his medical adviser was called in. "Sir," said the doctor, "you are overtaxing your strength in every way. You should go out with the hounds one day less each week; and you must reduce your allowance of wine. You are destroying the *coats* of your stomach." "Then, hang me, doctor, if I do not fight in out in my *waistcoat*," said the quaint, eccentric old baronet. And truly, medical science was baffled in this instance; for, instead of following the advice of the physician, he added another to his hunting days per week, and doubled his portion of wine, laughed at the doctor, and grew fat and strong. And let us add another story about Sir Harry. It speaks for his heart, and deserves to be told. He called at Hoo-green one day to return a bad five pound note which he had received from the innkeeper at his last visit. "I hope," he said, "that it will be no loss to you, and that you know from whom you received it?" "Oh yes! Sir Harry, it's all right; I took it from Mr. ———," he answered, naming a poor curate in the neighbourhood. They were standing by the fire, and Sir Harry had still the note in his hand. In an instant it was torn to fragments and in the flames, while he said, "Poor fellow! I can stand the loss of it better than he can; and see that you don't make him uncomfortable by telling him anything about it. He might feel uneasy at being in any way obliged to me;" and in another moment he was on horseback and galloping down the lane. Honour to the memory of this brave old baronet! In this one act, so beautifully done, there was a combination of pure benevolence and true delicacy of feeling which could not possibly be surpassed. It could not have been done more kindly; it could not have been done more gracefully. The heart of the wild huntsman was in its right place.

CHAPTER XXIV.

TRAVELLING was both a difficult and a dangerous operation in former days. We do not know when a direct communication by coach between Liverpool and London was first established; but we have been told that some sort of stage was started to Warrington and Manchester in the year 1767. We have indeed read in an old Liverpool *Chronicle*, January 21st, 1768, that John Stonehewer, a driver of the said stage, had broken his thigh by a fall from the box, a very likely accident in those old-fashioned days of rough stone pavements. Many of our readers must recollect with what persevering tenacity the shaking old road between Liverpool and Prescot was maintained as part and parcel of the British constitution, to the great loss and damage of our more modern coach proprietors, whose vehicles were more tried and injured by the eight miles of paving stones between these two towns than by all the rest of the journey to the metropolis. The surveyors stood by the paving stones to the last. Liverpool always adhered to the old ways, however rough they might be. Macadam, "the Colossus of roads," as some wit called him, was an innovator; what right had he to make improvements which would militate against the trade of coach-builders and menders? Macadam! What a short reign was his?

"Come like shadows; so depart!"

Hardly had he grasped his sceptre firmly in his hand, and persuaded the people to mend their ways, when another and a mightier magician waved his wand, and all was changed. George Stephenson and railways burst upon us, and Macadam's meteor flight was brought to a sudden close. The fast man gave way to the faster.

The first coach which we can ourselves recollect travelling by was of a very long shape, and moved at a very slow pace. Its destination was Birmingham, at which we ultimately, after many delays and dangers, managed to arrive. It had many "odoriferous names," as Mrs. Malaprop would say, among which "the cheap and nasty" was the most prominent and usual. The coachman was a fat man, with a low-crowned hat, and a large nosegay stuck in his button-hole, the very man, we should say, who sat for the picture of old Mr. Weller in *Pickwick*. What business he had to transact on the road! He seemed to be the universal agent for the universal affairs of all mankind, between town and town, and village and village. And what stoppages, not only at public-houses, but "here, there and everywhere," had the miserable passengers consequently to undergo! And what universal flirtations he used to carry on with the universal womankind who dwelt by the wayside! He appeared to have reached high pressure or breach-of-promise point with some inmate of every cottage on the road. And then when at last we reached Birmingham, into what universal fleadom we found that we had plunged when we went to bed! We have eschewed sleeping at Birmingham ever since. A Birmingham bed is a perfect "Cannibal Isle," with a more carnivorous population than can be met with in any part of the globe. There is even less danger of being devoured in New Zealand itself.

But a new era sprang up in the coaching business. The "Bang-up" was started for Birmingham, and the "Umpire" for London. Those were splendid conveyances compared with their slow moving predecessors, combining, as they did, speed, safety, regularity and comfort. They were literally the timekeepers for the several towns and villages through which they passed. They started to a moment, arrived at each stage to a moment, and reached their final destination to a moment. The regularity of the dial could not have been greater. We have heard of the man who boasted that his clock regulated the sun, and truly the old Umpire and Bang-up seemed to regulate the clock. But "where are they now?" An echo answers, "Where?" Enter, as we have said before, George Stephenson, and exit Bretherton. Railways came in and coaches went out. *Sic transit gloria mundi.* We are all for speed now. The march of improvement first became a run, then a gallop, and now it has increased into a flight, beating wings and the wind.

But, nevertheless, it was pleasant travelling in those old days, "All right," said the guard; smack went the whip; "off she goes!" What a team! How the bits of blood do their work! Even the experienced hands of the veteran Jehu can hardly tame their fire and check their speed. And now the horn blows, we dash into the market-place of some country town, to the delight of the congregated idlers and gazers of the place. What a bustle among the grooms and stable boys. Parcels are handed up and down; the smoking horses are unharnessed; fresh ones put to, all in less time than it takes to tell it. Off again! We sweep at speed past the village green, dogs barking, pigs squealing, geese hissing, children shouting, men huzzaing, women smiling. Through the winding pleasant lanes we go, with their lovely hedgerows on either side, the spire in the distance, the mansion in the park, the glorious old trees, the noble woods, the delicious lakes, the sparkling streams, altogether a landscape of sweetness and beauty which no country but merry England can set before the traveller's eye. All this, however, was lost to us when the last of the coaches disappeared from the road. We now fly, but we do not see. We are, as it were, shot forth from station to station at a speed becoming the spirit of the age. But one consequence of all this is, that the rising generation know nothing of the old high-ways and by-ways of their country, its many beauties, its shady lanes, its lovely nooks and corners, the sudden turns in our old lines of road which used unexpectedly to open to us the most charming prospect, and then as suddenly to hide it, only to reveal to us some other vision of beauty on the fair face of nature spread before us. These were exquisite treats to us old travellers. We miss them, but we are not regretting. We like to keep up with the pace of the age.

And what early hours our grandfathers and grandmothers used to keep! What an anarchical, chaotical, daring, radical innovator, the very *æs triplex circum pectus* man of old Horace, was that bold spirit considered to be amongst them who first wrote four o'clock, instead of mid-day, upon his "ticket for soup." Then came dinner at five, at six, and all hours, until day and night changed places, and late hours and indigestion became triumphant, until wise people learned that the best plan was to lay in a stock of solids at lunch, and then only trifle and coquet with the grand banquet of the evening.

But how different was the style of visiting in those days from what it is now. About five or six o'clock you might see the ladies on a visit to the house of some one of their number, who was giving what was called "a rout" to her female friends. We speak advisedly when we say her female friends, because it was as difficult to press a gentleman into the service on such occasions as to catch an ostrich or a real live rhinoceros. A treasure, indeed, was the man, and a star, and an idol, who would come to these parties. Dr. Gerard, once mayor of Liverpool, was an especial pet with the ladies in St. Anne-street for accepting all their invitations to these meetings. But what was a rout? It was a muster of all her female friends, with the *rara avis* of a gentleman, if, like Mrs. Glass's hare in the cookery book, one could be caught by the heroine or lady-hostess of the evening. The custom was to crowd as many guests as possible into a small room, or a large one, as the case might be. As the hour for assembling arrived, there was a tremendous crush of sedan-chairs towards the mansion where the party was given. There were several stands for these old-fashioned conveyances in Newington-bridge. Those ladies who were not so magnificent in their notions, or more moderate in their pocket, might be seen making their way to the festival with what were called calashes over their heads, a reduced form of the covering still raised over gigs on a rainy day. When the party, or a sufficient number to commence operations, had mustered, tea and coffee, rather weak than strong, and bread and butter, rather thin than thick, were handed round. This ceremony performed, the business of the evening fairly began. The lady of the house made up her card tables. Some would sit down to whist, of course, in those old days, long antediluvian patriarchal whist, silver threepences the stake, and nothing more. Short whist had not then come in, with gas, steam railways, and electric telegraphs. But the favourite game with the ladies was one called quadrille or preference. Perhaps they liked it better than whist because it was carried on with more talking. We never could fathom its mysteries. In truth, we never tried to dive into them. All that we recollect of it is, that it went on with a dreadful clamour about the " pool," " basting," " spadille," "manille," "ponto," and "basto;" some of which phrases sounded very like Egyptian hieroglyphics turned into language, while others had a sporting smack about them. Indeed we are not certain whether "ponto" is not altogether a fiction or confusion of our memory. When the lady of the house began to tire, or fancied that her company began to flag or look fatigued over their cards, she gave the signal, and in rushed the servants with the trays, on which were spread refreshments of a very mild and innocent character. Ices were almost unknown in those days. Weak lemonade and weaker negus, with jumbles and ratafia cakes, were handed round, and, as they were nibbled and sipped at, Mrs. Gildart would vow that she was nearly ruined by a run of bad luck, which had impoverished her to the amount of two-and-sixpence. Dr. Gerard would meekly affirm that he had had a most delightful evening. Robert Norris would lay his hand upon his heart, and swear that he was always at the service of the ladies. Beau Sealy, still, we are told, a flourishing and vigorous plant somewhere near Bridgewater, would smile one of his demure smiles, and say ditto to Norris, ditto to Gerard. The hostess was delighted; the ladies were in raptures. Who like Norris? Who like Gerard? Who, especially, like Sealy? Sealy being single, as he is single still. By this time all the nibbling and sipping were over. The jumbles, and cakes, and negus, and lemonade had disappeared. The candles were burning low. There was a cry for the calashes, and a rush to the sedans, and "the feast of reason and the flow of soul" were at an end for that evening. And all this happiness, recollect, was achieved before nine o'clock. Our mothers and grandmothers were unrobing for the night before their glasses at the hour at which our modern belles are sitting before theirs, clasping the sparkling necklace, arranging the last curl, and practising the fatal smile which is to do such execution at the Wellington-rooms or some private party. We will not attempt to decide upon the charms of the ancient and modern *Houris;* but the *hours* kept by the former were certainly more reasonable and seasonable. They had the advantage of all "the beauty sleep," which is said to come before midnight.

CHAPTER XXV.

HERE must be many old stagers still surviving amongst us who can remember the two managers of the Theatre Royal, Messrs. Knight and Lewis. The latter was the father of Mr. Thomas Lewis, so well known to the present and last generations. In *Tyke* and similar characters Knight was unequalled; while Lewis was the best *Mercutio* ever seen upon the stage. Both were gentlemen, and much liked in society. In those days, moreover, we had occasional visits from the celebrated John Kemble, and his as celebrated sister, Mrs. Siddons, when they were "starring it" in the provinces. Cooke, likewise, the predecessor of Kean in his peculiar line of characters, often appeared upon the Liverpool boards. He was not famous for his sobriety, and one night, being hissed for his usual sin, he rushed forward to the lights, and most unceremoniously told the audience that "he was not there to be insulted by a set of wretches, every brick in whose infernal town was cemented by an African's blood!" This was a home thrust for our grandfathers. For-

tunately for the offender, Lynch-law was unknown in those times, or he might have been the author and hero of a tragedy of his own.

And what glorious singers used to warble in our music-hall in those days! We can just remember them, although singing to us, in our babyhood and childhood, was very like "wasting their sweetness on the desert air." Among them were Incledon, Bartleman, Braham, the *semper florens*, then in his prime, if not ever since and always in his prime; Mrs. Billington, and, above all and before all, that wonder of the world, Catalani herself. It is something to say that we have heard this glorious songstress, although then quite unable to appreciate her spirit-stirring and soul-melting notes.

But we forgot to mention Elliston among our list of actors; eccentric, clever, well-educated, well-read, accomplished, amusing, gentlemanly Elliston. He was a prodigious favourite in Liverpool, as much so off as on the stage. He was ever a welcome guest at the tables of our merchant princes, and, by his powers of conversation and amazing fund of information, well repaid all the attentions which he received. His range of characters, both in tragedy and comedy, was a very extensive one. His performance in *Three and the Deuce* was the perfection of acting, and, however often repeated, never failed to command the rapturous applause of the theatre-going public of Liverpool. A pleasant, agreeable man was Elliston, full of fun, abounding in good stories, and with an encyclopædia of anecdotes at his command. He was somewhat proud of his profession, and his profession was proud of him. It lost nothing when represented in his person.

And now, as we bring our reminiscences to a conclusion, we must not omit to chronicle that, three times since memory and observation dawned within us, we have seen Liverpool overwhelmed by grief and sorrow. The first of these occasions was when the intelligence arrived of the death of Nelson, in achieving the greatest of his great victories, that of Trafalgar. As a sailor, and the chief of sailors, he was an especial favourite in this seaport town. His name was among our "household words." His life, a thousand romances in one reality, was the popular theme at every table, and round every fire. Wellington was in the bud then, and all the talk was of Nelson, Nelson, nothing but Nelson. When, therefore, the account of his death was received, there was not a man in Liverpool but wished with all his heart and soul that the battle had been unfought, and the victory unwon, and the departed hero yet alive and spared to us. It seemed, so intense was the feeling of regret, as if the destroying angel had again passed through the land, as of old through Egypt, and taken one from every house. Grief was in every family, lamentation in every circle, sorrow on every countenance. These feelings were the more intense in Liverpool, inasmuch as the intelligence of the hero's death followed close upon a letter from himself, in which he announced his intention, as he had never yet seen "the good old town," of paying it a visit, as soon as he had "settled his small account" with the French and Spanish fleets, which he was then blockading in Cadiz. How uncertain are the events of this life! We wept the hero dead, whom we hoped to welcome in all the pride and brilliancy of his glory! The envelope containing the letter in which the announcement alluded to was made, hung for many a long year, in a splendid frame, in the dining-room of Mr. J. B. Aspinall, of Duke-street. But there are hero-worshippers yet surviving, who look up to Nelson as their idol. A few months since we entered a cottage in a remote district, far from Liverpool. Our eye at once settled upon an autograph, framed and suspended against the wall. It was Nelson's handwriting. The owner of the house entered as we were gazing at it, and seeing how we were employed, remarked, "That is the greatest treasure I possess. Nothing on earth should separate me from it while I live." We looked at the man, who seemed not to have a spark of enthusiasm in his composition on any other subject; but, upon talking to him, we found that his whole soul was wrapped up in adoration of the memory of Nelson. We may not wonder, then, when such a feeling is found to exist now, at the burst of enthusiasm which echoed through the nation during the life, and at the death, of the popular idol; and what a subscription was raised for a monument to the mighty and fallen hero! And what collections were made in all our churches for the widows and orphans of the brave defenders of their country, who fought and were killed on the same day with their glorious chief! But Liverpool was never deaf to the call and inspirations of charity. To the poet's question,

> "Art thou content to be the modern Tyre,
> Half pedlar and half tyrant of the world?"

she may proudly and truly answer, that she has ever recognised and acted upon a loftier and nobler mission. Behold her Infirmary, her Blind Asylum, her Dispensaries, her Hospitals, her institutions of every kind, for every form and shape in which woe and want come upon mankind! Freely have her sons of many generations received, and freely have they given. They are not perfect, but selfishness has never been among their faults.

The second time when Liverpool, within our recollection, was struck with distress, but it was altogether of another character, was when the great West Indian merchant, George Bailey, failed. It was thought at the time that nobody could survive the shock. For a season all trade was checked, all credit and confidence paralysed, and "Who next?" was the question of every day in every mouth, as men walked about doubtingly on 'Change, and looked into every new *Gazette* with fear and trembling.

The third season of consternation to which we have alluded was the actual panic occasioned by the abolition of the African slave trade. Our whole community was terror-stricken, when the cause of philanthropy triumphed in Parliament, and it was decreed that England should no longer play a guilty part in perpetrating and perpetuating the horrors of the middle passage. When this was proclaimed in Liverpool, prophets of woe and evil sprung up in every street. Destruction was about to fall upon us, chaos was to come again, an *avalanche* was to overwhelm us, or an earthquake to swallow us up, grass was to grow in the area of the Exchange-buildings, our warehouses were to moulder into ruins, the streets were to be ploughed up, the docks were to become fish-ponds, and our mercantile navy, whose keels penetrate to every land, and whose white sails woo the breeze on every ocean, was to dwindle into a fishing vessel or two, or be utterly extinguished. It is true that there were some men amongst us of too sanguine or too sagacious a spirit to believe in these melancholy predictions. They had yet hope or faith in the development of the resources and energies of their townsmen. Among them we must place Mr. Shaw, of Everton, and Mr. Edward Houghton, of Great Nelson-street, both large holders of land in their respective neighbourhoods, who, influenced by an inward and assured conviction that Liverpool, cut off from one branch of trade, had yet a great future before her, calmly " bided their time," and waited for the period when the town would reach them, and building land at so much per yard would be the cry. Above all Mr. Leigh, the solicitor, one of the shrewdest men of his day, clung to this notion, and boldly speculated upon it. And the result has been, in his case, that his son, Mr. John Shaw Leigh, is one of the wealthiest, probably the wealthiest, commoner in England, able, as some one lately observed in his presence, " not only to buy up a duke, but half-a-dozen dukes, if they were in the market."

But these far-seeing men were the exceptions. Ruin to Liverpool was the general fear of her inhabitants upon the abolition of the slave-trade. We wonder now, when we look back, that England, and Englishmen, should ever have tolerated and sanctioned the nefarious traffic in human flesh. But, while the trade existed, it had champions and defenders, not only among those who were interested in it, but among classes whose blindness can only be attributed to prejudice, the offspring of habit and custom. Thus, Boswell, in his *Life of Johnson*, calmly writes, " The wild and dangerous attempt which has been for some time persisted in to obtain an act of our Legislature, to abolish so very important and necessary a branch of commercial interest, must have been crushed at once, had not the insignificance of the zealots who vainly took the lead in it made the vast body of planters, merchants, and others, whose immense properties are involved in the trade, reasonably enough suppose that there could be no danger. The encouragement which the attempt has received excites my wonder and indignation, and, though some men of superior abilities have supported it, whether from a love of temporary popularity, when prosperous, or a love of general mischief, when desperate, my opinion is unshaken. To abolish a *status*, which, in all ages, God has sanctioned, and man has continued, would not only be *robbery* to an innumerable class of our fellow-subjects, but it would be extreme cruelty to the African savages, a portion of whom it saves from massacre and intolerable bondage in their own country, and introduces into a much happier state of life, especially now when their passage to the West Indies, and their treatment there, is humanely regulated. To abolish this trade would be, to

> 'Shut the gates of mercy on mankind.'

Whatever may have passed elsewhere concerning it, the House of Lords is wise and independent.

> *Intaminatis fulget honoribus;*
> *Nec sumit aut ponit secures*
> *Arbitrio popularis auræ.*"

Such was the hollow and feeble sophistry of such men as Mr. James Boswell, and so fondly and foolishly did they talk.

But not of his opinion was our own noble and immortal Roscoe, who devoted a long life to the cause of philanthropy, and battled for freedom for the slave in every variety of ways, beginning with his poem of "Mount Pleasant," and ending with his vote for abolition in the House of Commons. But not of his opinion were the Wilberforces, and Clarksons, and Macaulays, and Croppers, and Rathbones, and Rushtons, and Curries, who fought the great battle of outraged humanity, at first, against mighty and tremendous odds, but still struggling on,

> "Like a thunder-cloud streaming against the wind."

until the *popularis aura*, public opinion, pronounced

in their favour. Then was heard the *sic volo, sic jubeo*, of the British people ; and truly, in this instance, we may say it was *vox populi, vox Dei*. Justice triumphed. The foulest blot which ever darkened the name of England was removed. The slave-trade was abolished. And what became of Liverpool ? Were the melancholy predictions of her prophets fulfilled ? Were her docks turned into fish-ponds ? Did the mower cut hay, or the reaper gather in his harvest, in her deserted streets ? Look round, and see. Compare what she was then with what she is now. Then we counted her inhabitants by tens, now by hundreds, of thousands. Then we talked of her acres, now of her miles, of docks. New channels of commerce sprung up, new fields of adventure and enterprise were discovered in the East and the West, and the far off South. Steam gave an additional impulse to the gigantic energies of trade, the manufacturing districts soared to the miraculous point of prosperity which they have attained, and Liverpool was the main artery through which all the imports and exports of these busy hives of industry unceasingly flowed.

What a different place the town is now from what it was when first we old stagers knew it, and were acquainted with every face which flitted through its streets ! So changed, so altered is it ! Old streets and old buildings gone, and new ones occupying their places ; streets where once were fields ; docks where of old were strand, and shore, and forts, and baths; retired villages swallowed up by the insatiable and still growing town ; trees, gardens, meadows, corn land, all yielding to the spread of brick and mortar. So marvellous are all these things, that, as we wander through the transmuted scene, losing and finding our way by turns, we know not how to describe the feelings which swell within us;

> "We see, we recognise, and almost deem
> The present dubious, or the past a dream!"

And what of the future of Liverpool? Has she reached the meridian height of her glory and prosperity? or is she yet in her dawn and beginning? Shall we moralise upon the fate of Tyre, of Carthage, of Genoa, and Venice, and other marts of commerce in bygone days? It was not for such a purpose that we took up our pen. We do not aspire to be prophets. But as yet no cloud is in the sky. All is bright and clear above the horizon; all is fair, promising, hopeful. And when we contemplate "the good old town," in which we have spent so many happy years, and to which we are bound by so many ties of friendship and affection, we take leave of her with the prayer of the Italian for his country—

"ESTO PERPETUA."

www.ingramcontent.com/pod-product-compliance
Lightning Source LLC
Chambersburg PA
CBHW020840160426
43192CB00007B/722